# UNDER
# HIS
# WINGS
## THE GOD OF MIRACLES AND FIRE

# DEBORAH WILLIAMS
FOREWORD BY JENNIFER A. MISKOV, Ph.D.

Published by Deborah Williams
Made in the USA

Copyright © 2018, Deborah Williams

Cover design and interior design:
David A. Stoddard - mediarevelation.com

978-1983982019
1983982016

Address:
Deborah Williams
2378 Columbia Way
Redding, CA 96003

Email: deborahwil49@gmail.com
Website: deborahunderhiswings.com

UNDER HIS WINGS
(PSALM 91:4)
DEBORAH'S BOOK

# DEDICATION

I am dedicating this book to my father Newton, my mother Helen who left a legacy of faith for me to follow, my husband Chris Benson for supporting and encouraging me to pursue my dreams, to my children Monica, Juliet, Hazel, David, their spouses George, Dennis, my grandchildren, my great grandchildren, and my mentor Dr. Jennifer A. Miskov who inspired me to write this book through her *Writing In The Glory* book and workshops.

I am the most blessed woman. I have learned so much from them. Their love for life has been an inspiration and delight to me. I pray that they will always keep their love for God and for each other at their forefront.

Special "Gammy" love for my six grandchildren and six great grandchildren. I pray that the Spirit of faith will increase in their lives and that they will be single eyed, Jesus at the center of it all, God personally going with them. In the Presence of the Lord is strength for the journey.

# ENDORSEMENTS

Deborah is a true disciple of Jesus and knows how to obey the Word of the Lord in Matthew 28:19 Off you go, make disciples of all nations. Deborah has literally fulfilled this directive with courage, boldness, fearlessness and love. For the reader, you will be challenged, encouraged, transformed and matured as you encounter Jesus in Deborah's life. You will learn lessons in trust, generosity, faith, love, prosperity, longsuffering, grace and forgiveness. I Congratulate Deborah on "A Great Read."

Rev. Judith Gates
Senior Pastor and founder of The Blessing Church
Sydney
New South Wales, Australia

Deborah Williams is incredible! She is the real deal! From humble beginnings, this young woman was swept into an unstoppable love story which has taken her around the world to see impossibilities bow to the name of Jesus. It is a story which reveals the extravagant and unquenchable love of her maker. A prophetic story which you will find yourself in. As you read these raw accounts, you can't help but to be inspired that Jesus wants to do the same with you! Just like Deborah, You were not created to shape history alone; rather you were created to LIVE "*Under His Wings*" and change the world. If you are hungering for more of God, I want to challenge you, read this book and then lean back into the covering of His love and say "Jesus do it again with me!"

Praying RADICAL FAVOR OVER THIS BOOK!
Jesus may you raise up 1000 more like Deborah!!!

Dave Harvey
Director Global Legacy
Bethel Church
Redding California

Deborah is one of a kind. Her heart is soft and tender while at the same time burning for souls. Her life is a testimony, because she has been set apart by Jesus Christ. As you read the testimonies throughout this book, allow them to stir up a hunger inside of you. I am very proud of Deborah because she has been persistent and has never given up throughout her life. She has made a commitment not to retire but to stay on fire for Jesus. I love being around Deborah, because she is a woman of faith. Faith is what attracts God's attention. As you read these testimonies, allow God's faith to grow in your heart and to believe that anything is possible through God. I personally, love and value Deborah as a mother in the faith. I believe in the call of God that is on her life.

Chris Overstreet,
International Evangelist and Conference Speaker,
Founder of Compassion To Action.
Bethel Church
Redding California

Deborah is a friend of God. She knows her God and her God knows her. Here is one who has laid down her all for the sake of Christ and His kingdom. *Under His Wings* is a living testimony of her intimacy with Jesus, courageous faith, unrelenting pursuit of the Spirit's presence and power, and compassion for the lost and hurting. This inspiring book will stir your heart and ruin your life for the ordinary!

Dr. Cornelius Quek
Founder, 7K &
Elisha's Room
Redding California

I first met Deborah Williams about ten years ago when she was invited as a special guest speaker to a Friday night Bible study group. Deborah showed great love and compassion to my wife who was struggling with various traumatic issues. We called upon Deborah to help us numerous times when we were in deep distress and she was always welcoming of us and invited us to her home to have times of worship and prayer. Over the years we have become good friends and are extremely grateful for Deborah's continued spiritual counsel and help.

I am greatly honoured to be asked to write an endorsement for Deborah's book – *"Under His Wings God of Miracles and Fire"*. What Deborah went through is quite amazing and wonderful to read, inspiring me in so many ways: for example, to forgive people who have treated me badly and to trust God in all circumstances. Deborah's life is one of worship and intimacy with God. If you love to hear stories of the marvellous ways God intervenes and turns impossible situations around, of God's love reaching out to heal and set people free, you will love reading Deborah's book. Be inspired and encouraged!

Gautham Jayachandran
Lab Manager
Discipline of Biomedical Science
University of Sydney
New South Wales
Australia

In reading Deborah's generous and grace filled words you will be inspired and challenged with a powerful perspective on the nature and goodness of God. Her passionate pursuit of Jesus is a rich treasure to be mined by all those who wish to fulfill their own destiny.

Ben Armstrong
Prophetic Ministry Director
Bethel Church, Redding California

# ACKNOWLEDGEMENTS

Without the constant empowering of the Holy Spirit, this book would never have been written. He inspired, directed, and energized me all the way through. Therefore all the glory must go to God for the ways in which He will use the contents.

My beloved husband and best friend, Christopher Charles Benson and I have worked on this project together. With God's enablement Chris has done all the word processing on the computer. His prayers, patient listening, re-reading and wise responses have also been invaluable.

My special thanks to the Bethel Church in Redding California for prophesying over me to write the book when I first visited, Jennifer A. Miskov, for your labor of love in inspiring me to actually write the book and editing my manuscript. David Stoddard, one of the most kind and patient men I know, for designing the book cover and formatting the book. Gautham Jayachadran for the proof reading. Kathy Dombrowski the manager of the Home of Peace built for healing and refreshments for missionaries in Oakland California, for allowing me to give birth to the first chapters of this book on the desk of the great woman of God Carrie Judd-Montgomery the Revivalist, the founder of the Home of Peace. This would have been near impossible without you guys.

I am deeply indebted and grateful to my daughters Monica, Juliet, Hazel, my son-in-law George, my Pastor Judith Gates of The Blessing Church family, Pastor Bernadette Nahlous and all the intercessor friends who diligently prayed us through. I was conscious that God was answering their prayers.

It was a delight to work with Abby Alderman, Dale Lawrence and Andrew Clark in editing. They were so cooperative and sensitive to this author's needs, which are greatly appreciated.

Deborah Willams

# CONTENTS

# FOREWORD

*The God of Miracles and Fire*

Deborah's life, faith, and testimonies will stir a great hunger inside of you to pursue God at all costs. Her journey through hardships, disappointments, betrayal, and loss and how she kept her eyes on Jesus throughout it all, will inspire great hope and healing to your heart. Her resilience and ability to forgive and move forward despite hardship releases great courage to remain in God no matter what the circumstances.

The God of Miracles and Fire is truly the God of Deborah Williams. In the same way that she has experienced God like this, she also brings an encounter with these similar characteristics of her Father in heaven. Written with raw vulnerability and honesty, Deborah takes you on a journey into her heart and releases keys that have helped her make it through devastating circumstances only to come out stronger, more courageous, and more on fire for Jesus.

There is something profound and beautiful about stewarding the stories and victories of God in our lives. The power of the testimony and the breakthroughs of yesterday are not just meant to be memories that have come and gone. These prophesy into a greater future and destiny. They reveal deeper secrets of the heart of God for what lies ahead. Remembering His faithfulness in the past is like activating a slingshot to propel us into the future with momentum for even greater freedom, breakthrough, encounters, and miracles. Not only that, these testimonies also release impartation for any and all who receive them to grab hold of them as seeds of faith for God to do a similar miracle again. These signs and wonders of the past simply foreshadow greater triumphs to come.

*Under His Wings* is filled with testimony after testimony of God's miraculous power and breakthrough. You can't help but get inspired and full of faith when reading this book. I pray that all who read this receive the fullness of the gift that Deborah is offering by sharing her story. May Deborah's ceiling become your floor. May her lifelong example of what it looks like to be a burning one for Jesus and to not burn out, kindle a fire inside of you that only increases it's flames with age. I pray that you would burn for Jesus all the days of your life and be consumed by His overshadowing and fiery love. As you live and not die in this world of options, may you remain focused on His face and realize that in intimacy and communion with God, you too would know the God of miracles and fire like never before. As you remain steadfast in Him no matter what storms come your way, I bless you with fresh fire from heaven. He never fails and His pursuit for your heart is like a burning flame. We were born for passion. May you be ruined for anything less than His fiery love.

Place me like a seal over your heart,
like a seal on your arm;
for love is as strong as death,
its jealousy unyielding as the grave.
It burns like blazing fire,
like a mighty flame.
Song of Solomon 8:6 (NIV)

Jennifer A. Miskov, Ph.D., Author and
Founding Director of Destiny House
www.silvertogold.com

# INTRODUCTION

## MY GOAL FOR THIS BOOK

My heart's desire is that through this book Jesus' name may be lifted up in all the earth, so that everyone may know that He alone is the Lord, the Most High God over all creation. I believe now is the time to write the book. I want to write it to give God the glory for what He has done. It will release faith for the impossible to those who read it.

My prayer is that everyone who reads *Under His Wings* will hunger and thirst for the presence of God, surrender their lives to knowing God more and more, and never be satisfied by anything that this world can offer, even at its best. Let us go into deeper levels of intimacy with Jesus and never get enough.

Jesus' love is matchless and beautiful. I am ruined for the ordinary. I surrender. I want to know Jesus more and more. His glory is what I long for. Nothing else matters, my deepest longing and desire is to sit at His feet, delight His heart in worship and give Him all the glory. I love You Jesus, with all that I am. My heart and soul are Yours and You are all I hope to be.

This is a book about a life lived in obedience to Jesus with signs and wonders experienced as a result. It explains the many lessons I have learned throughout my life. My secret has been doing what Mary said (John 2:5), "Whatever He tells you to do, do it." My heart's desire is to stir up hearts to believe for the impossible!

# CHAPTER 1

# A HUMBLE BEGINNING

When I first visited Bethel Church in Redding, California, in 2013, I was given a prophetic word: "Deborah, the Lord is saying, 'It's time to write the book." Many people had told me that I should write a book, but that prophetic word started me on the journey of wanting to do it. I thought I would be able to start writing straightaway, but like all things with God, timing is very important. I didn't know how I was going to do it or even where to start, so I went back to Australia pondering how I was going to begin. The following year I again felt led to visit Bethel and the International House of Prayer (IHOP). But when I attempted to book my tickets, the travel schedule and cost would not allow for me to come to Bethel first. My travel agent said, "Deborah, if you go to IHOP first, it will be cheaper." I said, "I don't know why the Lord is not allowing my plans to work, but you can book me the way it's working out." And so he did. After the tickets were booked, I went online to check what was happening at IHOP and found out that two days after I arrived, there would be a prophetic conference. Additionally, the day I arrived at Bethel, the Healing School conference would begin. How faithful is our Daddy.

He didn't want me to miss out on any of it. So He arranged things in such a way that would fit just right.

After the first session of the prophetic conference at IHOP, the coordinator asked me to have lunch with her. When we went back for the second session, she said to the delegates, "I have just had lunch with my beautiful friend, a pastor from Australia, and she is going to take this session to share her love for Jesus with us." I thought, "Wow, Lord, You could have at least prepared me for this beforehand." Well, there was no time to debate. I was given the microphone and shared from my heart my love for Jesus, the Lover of my soul. There was no dry eye in the place. One lady called out, "This is so beautiful, but you have got us all crying. I want that!" I was asked again to speak during the last session and again, the Lord did a beautiful work in the hearts of all who were there.

The next day we were divided into small groups for the prophetic booths. To my surprise, one of the prophetic words given to me was, "I see you surrounded by a lot of young people. You are being a mother to them." At the time I thought, "Well, Lord, in our church we have young people, but not as many as the ones prophesied." Regardless, I recorded it and pondered it in my heart. Two days later, I was on my way to Bethel. The day I arrived, I attended the Healing School conference. During the last day of the conference, the building was believed to be on fire and we were all sent outside. The fire brigade came and searched for the fire but could not find one. As we waited outside, I met a lady who became a good friend. She invited me to have lunch with her and then took me to her house, where I was warmly welcomed by her husband. After the Sunday morning service, they offered to take me on their beautiful boat at Whiskeytown Lake. They said I could bring friends if I wanted to, so I invited some friends from Bethel Church whom I had met during my first and second visits. I had a wonderful time lying on the sofa, watching these friends who had never met before chatting and getting along so beautifully. I felt like a mother at Christmas, watching her children who had come home for the holidays. I thanked the Lord for using me to connect these friends.

That evening, we attended the Sunday night service. I was called out again and prophesied over. As I stood in front with other hungry worshippers, all of a sudden I found myself saying to the Lord, "It would be lovely to come here and stay for a while just to worship You with these people." I didn't think it would be possible, as I had just spent my money on that holiday. Yet in that moment, I found myself desiring to attend the Bethel School of Supernatural Ministry (BSSM), even though I had already completed five years of ministry training and had been an ordained minister of the gospel for years. I didn't even know if they accepted older people into the school. After the service, I asked to receive prayer for the desire in my heart. As I was going out of the door with a friend, she said to a young man standing there, "Please pray for this Australian pastor; she is hungry and wants to go to school here." The young man took my hand and prayed for me and he said, "Sister, I have just seen someone putting $6,000 in your hands. You are going to have no problem getting the money to come." So I went home to Australia and spoke to my senior pastor. She said, "Deborah, if it was any other college I would say that you didn't need it. But because it's Bethel, I will say yes." There was already someone I had been mentoring who could take my pastoral role, so I applied and was accepted to attend BSSM the following September.

The third and final year of school was spent interning for Dr. Jennifer Miskov, author of *Writing in the Glory*, as well as several other books. At the time that it was prophesied that, I would be surrounded by many young people, I didn't know how it was going to happen, as we didn't have that many young people in our church. But now here I am, surrounded by young people and enjoying the privilege of being a spiritual mother. I have grown so much through my experience of the Father's love and goodness. He has been so gracious to me and has good things in store for me. I have received a deep revelation of Dad's love and nature. He is taking me from glory to glory. His presence changes everything. I am feeding myself on what He is feeding on. I have expectancy regarding the promises. I am an intimate participant in worship. He kisses me on my forehead and says, "I love you." From that affection, I carry something from the wind of the Spirit. I have seen God do many amazing things since I have been here. I have seen many healed, delivered, born again, and filled with the Holy Spirit. I have had opportunities to go on mission trips to different nations and see Him work there as well.

I am ready and willing to share my life story because I believe that it will encourage and inspire others to believe God and His word. I serve the God who cannot fail or lie. He changes seasons, but He does not change (Malachi 3:6). I want others to know that our past does not dictate nor determine our redeemed future. God's purpose for our lives will stand the tests of life if we yield our lives to Him and let Him take control. I have chosen to yield and live a surrendered life. I have let go of all that is of myself and of all control to go on a life journey of discovery with the One who has endless affection for me. So I say, "Jesus, take my hand and lead me on!"

# CHAPTER 2

# PAINFUL YEARS

The early years of my life were very difficult. I was born in what is known today as Zimbabwe. I lived with my parents until I was three years of age, but over the next four years, my mother was very sick. I do not know what was wrong; I was too young to know. All I heard them say was that she was in a lot of pain. I remember the last time I visited her in the hospital; my sweet sister-in-law, Rosemary, brought me along with her. I did not get to see my mum's face because when we got there she was fast asleep. The nurse said, "She has been in a lot of pain and we have just settled her. It is better not to wake her up." Soon after, she was released so that she could die in the comfort of her home. That very night she passed on. I remember her funeral and the hymns they sang. They come alive in difficult times. They bring so much comfort to me. I can remember every word of those songs, such as "Rock of Ages." To this day, these words will still suddenly come to me during times of hardship.

After the death of my mother I lived with my stepmother, who was a very cruel woman. Because of this treatment, I determined in my heart that I was going to be kind to people. My stepmother used to starve me and treat me like a slave. I had to carry water with a big bucket from a well that was too far to go for such a little one. She used to get me up early to make fire to heat the house and to heat water for breakfast. She gave me porridge without sugar and no lunch for school. After school, she would send me to work in other people's fields for little pay, and at dusk I had to go and gather my father's cattle from the bush without shoes. At one point, my feet became infected, but she showed no mercy and still had me doing everything. My father worked away from home, as he owned a hotel in another part of the country. We were not a poor family; we lived in a brick house while others lived in mud houses. I should have had a good life, but because of my stepmother's cruelty, I grew up like a child from a poor family. My father didn't know about any of this because I was afraid of what my stepmother would do if I told him how she was treating me.

When I was nine years old, I was given a hiding for something that I didn't do. I ran into the bush and began to cry. I found a rock shaped like a stump, hugged it and cried into it saying, "Lord, if my mum were alive, I wouldn't be suffering the way I am now." All of a sudden, peace came over my heart. From that day, I learned that if I call out to God, He would hear me and help me. It was comforting even though I didn't know how He was going to do it. But somehow I knew I was going to be all right.

That's when my history with God really began. He gave me faith to believe. I learned to cry to God at a young age. I first experienced His love in an open field and throughout the years, His love has not changed.

### *The Lord made "a way of escape" (Exodus 14:30)*

The following year the Lord made a way for me by sending me to live with my brother Miles and his wife Rosemary for a year. My brother was the headmaster of the local primary school.

They were both very kind to me, but my sister-in-law was also a no-nonsense type of person. She kept everything very clean and taught me how to do things right the first time so that I could go play and not have to do them again. Their door was always open; no one was a stranger to them. Everyone was made to feel welcome and there was always food to eat and a bed to sleep in. If people arrived unexpectedly, Rosemary would without hesitation give them the food she had already prepared for us and would continue cooking until we all had had something to eat. She modeled generosity for me, something that I still remember to this day.

I aged out of my brother's primary school at the end of the year and returned home to start boarding school. I came to my brother's house beaten down and weary, but left feeling loved and full of hope for the life ahead of me.

CHAPTER 3

# MY APPRECIATION TO THE ANGLICAN CHURCH

*Saint Anne's Mission*

I am very grateful to the Anglican Church mission that brought the gospel to my people before I was even born. They built a very good school where I received my education and I was taken to church as a child. I am thankful for the Sunday school teachers who shared the gospel with the other children and me. I gave my heart to Jesus at the age of seven in Sunday school, which was the same year my mum died. I don't remember much about her, but the hymns that were sung at her funeral became the pillar in my life that led to my conversion to Jesus Christ. They are still a source of encouragement to me in hard times.

When I became of age for boarding school, my stepmother tried to prevent me from going because to her, I was still her slave. Thankfully my father stepped in and said, "If she wants to go to boarding school, then to boarding school she will go." I am very grateful for the headmistress of the school, Miss Sweeting. She made many sacrifices, including laying down marriage, to be a missionary to my people and school. She didn't just teach us Arithmetic and English; she taught us important basic life skills, such as proper manners, hygiene, sewing, and cooking. Miss Sweeting was very strict, but was also very kind. She wanted us to be the very best that we could be in every area of our lives. We learned the importance of doing things right the first time and doing them well, helping us understand what it meant to be trustworthy and dependable. Miss Sweeting showed us how to honor and respect one another in a way that honored the Lord.

I enjoyed the days I spent in boarding school. Many people don't realize how important the formative years of a child's life truly are and that what happens to children when they are young will, in most cases, affect the rest of their lives. For example, children who are brought up with negativity spoken over them lack confidence even if they have the ability to do things, unless they meet someone who takes the time to pull the best out of them. Having teachers who can identify the strengths and weaknesses in children can help to develop and encourage children to grow in those areas, even if they don't get the same encouragement at home. It can make all the difference in a child's life. I know with certainty that it made a great difference in my life. I would think of what was said about me at Sunday school and at school, and about what was said about me at home. I would look at my schoolwork and see that I was not as stupid as I was always being made to feel at home. I would encourage myself by dreaming of the day that I would leave home, go away to boarding school, and eventually go to other nations to see how they lived their lives, something I always had a desire to see, especially as I learned more and more about the world in geography.

Nonetheless, I did my best to do things right at home, as we were taught at school, so that I could please my stepmother. But my stepmother would always find ways of belittling me. She always told me that I was stupid and would never amount to anything. But I would tell myself, "I am not stupid; I am going to prove you wrong.

I am going to be kind to people, like my grandma and sister-in-law."
They were good models for me. I loved going to spend holidays with
them. I didn't know then just how important and good it was, for me
to keep up that self-talk and positivity. Today, we call these declarations. If someone had told me that in my younger days, I would have
increased the volume and may have been a giant in the faith today.
But I am getting there. So, if you have been self-talking in a good
way, don't stop. Increase your daily intake! The negative words spoken over you will lose their grip as you stop paying attention to them
and fill your mind with the truth of God's Word. You will change
your life and the lives of those around you.

# CHAPTER 4

# THE INFLUENCE OF KINDNESS

*Leave a Legacy of Faith and Generosity*

My mum and her sister both died leaving young children be-hind. During my boarding school holidays, I stayed with Miles and Rosemary, and sometimes with my maternal grandmother. She was a sweet and godly woman who taught me a lot about life, especially about generosity. She, like Rosemary, was one of the most generous women I have ever known.

With Grandma, there was no competition; everyone was her favorite. Nothing was ever too much for her. I have very happy memories of the days that I was able to spend with her. On the day she died, we were called into her room to pay our respects. Incred-ibly, she had already died but had come back to life shortly thereaf-ter. She told us that she had been to heaven and was met at the gate by her two daughters, dressed in white and with the Lord behind them. She said that they asked her, "Mum, if you come now, who is going to look after the children?" Grandma told them, "I am now too old and am going blind; I am no longer able to look after them.

So I have asked the Lord to be allowed to go." With those words, she closed her eyes and passed away. We believed that the Lord granted her request to go home to be with Him. Looking back, I see how much Grandma did for us by modeling what it is to live and leave a legacy for future generations. I will always treasure it and pray that I leave the same legacy of faith and generosity.

After Grandma's death, I went back to the boarding school. Upon finishing school, I started my first job working with the Catholic nuns. As I had learned generosity from my family, I spent all of my first salary check on gifts for them; I did not spend a single penny on myself. I was very happy to have the opportunity to show my gratitude for what they had done for me.

*God's Intervention*

When I was 21 years old, the enemy tried to kill and destroy me (John 10:10). I was rushed to hospital with a lot of pain in my stomach. The doctors did a lot of tests, but could not find the cause of pain. One morning after two weeks, there were fifteen doctors surrounding my bed, but were unable to diagnose my condition. A few of them had suggested to cut me open to see what was wrong with me, but I had refused to sign the consent paper to go ahead with the operation. This put me in a potentially dangerous situation. At that time, we were living in Rhodesia (currently known as Zimbabwe) under the apartheid. The doctors threatened to put me out of the hospital and send me away sick, which they had the power to do. By then, I was so sick I could not even take myself to the bathroom. My personal anguish was overwhelming, but I never lost sight of God's goodness. He turned my circumstances around through a young doctor, who released life more abundantly in me. This doctor suggested to the others that they try a new tablet on the market. They started me on the tablet the same day. Within a week, I was much better and the pain went away. God made a way for me to live again.

I continued to work and to educate myself. After working for the Catholic nuns, I worked in a bank for a time. I found that I liked working with people, so I got a job working as a nurse until I got married. I met my husband through his uncle who worked with me. The Lord blessed us with two beautiful daughters, Monica and Juliet. Their father was a good husband and a good father to my children, but he had very controlling parents, especially his mother. She was a mean, manipulative woman. She didn't want my sister-in-law or me to live with our husbands where they worked, nor did she want us living in their village. She became jealous if my husband and brother-in-law bought anything for me or for my sister-in-law.

Whenever my husband sent me a parcel or money, she would open the parcel and take what she wanted giving me whatever was left. She was even jealous of her own daughters and what they had. All her children died around her. She kept my children away from me and wouldn't let me be with them. She didn't want me to see them or give them clothes or money. She tried to poison them against me by telling them lies. I thank God for their auntie, who was a kind woman and liked me; we lived in the same city. She was my point of contact and would take whatever I had for my daughters and send it to them. Through God's goodness and this woman's kindness, I was able to maintain a good relationship with my children and with the auntie until she died. What the enemy tried to use for evil, God used for good. I forgave my mother-in-law just as I forgave my step-mother. I have a healthy relationship with my children, which is all that matters to me.

## *My Little Family*

I am a blessed woman. I can truly say that my daughters have faith like their mother. The Lord has protected them through various trials and has shown them His love and grace. Juliet passionately loves the Lord. She was involved in a car accident in which four people died in 2008. She suffered a terrible leg injury, but God has done a wonderful healing work in her. Through life's challenges, Juliet always finds ways to praise the Lord and lives a contented life. Her life's Scripture verse is Philippians 4:12, which says: "I know both how to have a little and how to have a lot. In all circumstances I have learned the secret of contentment, whether well fed or hungry, whether in abundance or in need." She is always smiling and encouraging others. She is like a breath of fresh air. Nothing is too much for her. When asked how she is doing when she faces challenges, she always says, "I am alright. I am alive and all is going to turn out well."

Monica also has a rock solid faith. Her life Scripture is Psalm 23. She says "Even in the shadow of death He is with me." I remember once that she had to be rushed to the hospital for an operation for gallstones and a hernia. In the recovery room, after the drowsiness had gone, she said, "Thank God I am healed in Jesus' name. I thank the Lord, for He has done great things for me." Instead of complaining about pain, she praised the Lord. She is married to a wonderful husband, Dennis. They have three children, Cathy, Blessed, and Lacyleen, and have five grandchildren, Lowain, Larry, Brendon, Kalley and Leanne.

Four and half years later, I got married again and had another beautiful daughter, Hazel Shane. One day, Hazel came home from school with sore feet. She had caught plantar warts from the swimming pool, so I took her to the doctor. The doctor said, "She will need an appointment to get them burned." She said to me, "Mum, I don't want them to burn my feet. You and I will pray and God will take them away." I said, "Yes, I agree. Let's pray and before you go to bed, I will put Band-Aids on the warts. Let's pray that when you get up tomorrow, they will be stuck on the Band-Aids." Sure enough, in the morning, when I took off the Band-Aids, all the warts had fallen off her feet. We praised and thanked the Lord together. Another time, she had tonsillitis and the doctor said, "Her tonsils have gotten too big and need to be removed." She said, "Mum, I don't want to have an operation. Can we pray that the Lord will heal me?" We prayed together and again the Lord healed her. It's so wonderful when children grow up seeing God answer their prayers. Hazel's favorite Scriptures growing up were Psalm 4:8 and Ephesians 5:19. When she would soak in the bubble bath, we would hear her singing Ephesians 5:19: "Making melody in my heart, making melody in my heart, making melody in my heart unto the King of kings. Worship and adore Him. Worship and adore Him. Making melody in my heart unto the King of kings." Before she went to sleep, it was Psalm 4:8: "I will lie down in peace and sleep. For You alone O Lord make me dwell in safety." Hazel is married to a man named George, who is a wonderful and generous man of God and is like more than seven sons to me. They and their children, Brittany, Joel Daniel, Corey, and Nicky, have had their share of challenges, but each one of their children has experienced a miracle.

In 2016, when Hazel applied for Monica and Juliet to go to Australia, she was given a time frame when their visas would be ready and booked their tickets. When the visas did not arrive on time, she contacted the embassy. The lady whom she spoke with was rude and told Hazel that they had to wait. So they waited. When it was time to go on their trip, they packed their luggage and turned up at the embassy to pick up their visas. They met the woman whom Hazel had spoken to over the phone and found her to be very unsympathetic to their situation. She said, "It's your fault; you should not have booked your ticket until you had gotten your visas." Our entire family began to pray for the Lord to move in this situation. When I called for an update, Monica said, "Mum, the devil is a liar and we are getting on that plane. We are in line to board before we get to the end of the line, we are going to have our visas." Sure enough, before they got to the front of the line, Cathy, Monica's daughter, called and told them that the embassy had emailed the visas. So they got on the plane and flew to Australia. The devil was indeed proved to be a liar.

# UNDER HIS WINGS

## *You Never Get Lonely When You Are Generous*

I have always done my best to be very kind to people. Generosity takes your eyes away from self and causes you to see the needs of others. It causes you to count your blessings and want to share with others. I had a big house that was always full of kids. On Sundays, my husband and I never had a meal alone; we always found people to join us after a church service. I felt the Lord wanted us to invite people to our home who would not be able to invite us back, similar to how He shows us kindness that we cannot repay.

Later on, I felt the Lord wanted us to bless underprivileged children, so we started fostering children from the orphanage. I loved them and treated them just like my own. We also adopted Grandma Mary, a Scottish lady from a retirement village. She never married but dedicated her life to bring up her sister's children when her sister died young. When these children were grown up with good jobs, they grew distant with her. Hence, she loved spending her weekend in our house, joining us on holidays, and going to church with us. We did that for years until she died at 89 years of age.

CHAPTER 5

# IT'S AMAZING
# WHO GOD USES

In the 1970s, God used some of my ex-Catholic friends to introduce me to the Holy Spirit. During that time in my country, the services in the Catholic Church were in Latin. So I invited one of my friends to come with me to my Anglican church because the services were in the language everyone could understand. My friend was very smart and said, "Yes, I will come with you, and next week you come with me to my church." Wanting to win her to the Lord, I said, "Yes, I will come with you next week."

She didn't tell me that she and her sisters were now going to a different church until the following Sunday when she came to pick me up. She took me to her new church, which happened to be in the midst of a revival. She told me on the way that this church was a bit different than my church and the Catholic Church. She told me about how this church had helped her and her sisters with the problems they were having in their new house, which is how they started going there. One of the sisters worked with a girl who attended church and had helped them out. We got there half an hour early, but it was already packed. When the worship started, the presence of God became tangible almost immediately. There were several sick people, some even brought by ambulance from the hospital, who had come to receive healing and were restored during the worship without anyone laying hands on them. My heart was moved and I found myself wanting more of God.

The following weekend I went back to my Anglican Church and asked to be released with a blessing, which they did, though they said they were sad to see us go. We then joined the Assemblies of God Church. A week later, I was baptized in water, as I had only been sprinkled on the head as a child in the Anglican Church.

Midweek, I was invited to go to a home group, and that night I was baptized in the Holy Spirit and spoke in tongues. It felt like fire was coming out of my ears. I saw people praying and singing in the spirit so beautifully; I knew I had a tiny little stream. I was so thirsty for the rivers of living water to flow, I would get up early in the morning and pray fervently with my short spiritual language. One morning I was crying for more, then I burst into new languages I had not had before and a spiritual song began to flow. I continued to ask for more and rivers continued to flow. I was filled with unspeakable joy and praises to the Lord. I went to church on cloud nine as it was Sunday. The spiritual baptism touched me deeply. This experience brought me satisfaction in ways I had not previously experienced. It created a hunger for more of the Word of God and a freedom from fear of man, that is what people think of me. The church was growing fast and a few months later they were looking for another home to host a home group, so we offered ours. The two women who led that home group became my spiritual mothers. They moved in the power of the Holy Spirit and were women of prayer and loved the Word of God. I learned a lot from them and soon also fell in love with the Word and with prayer, thanks to their example.

One early Sunday morning, I had a dream in which the Lord showed me how to forgive my stepmother and my cousin who had been unkind to me. The Lord walked me through it, step by step. When I woke up, I asked the Lord if that was what I was to do.

He said, "Yes, you need to do that before you go to church and take communion. Follow the steps in the dream." And so I did. I forgave my stepmother and went to my cousin. When I saw her, there was no more pain in my heart. As I hugged her, she asked me to forgive her. We wept in each other's arms like nothing had ever happened. I saw the beauty of forgiving those who have hurt you, even when you were defenseless. I had thought I had already forgiven them, but it had been only superficial. Once the Lord walked me through it, my broken heart was healed. After that, I went to church and took communion. My life was radically changed forever. Thank You, Lord, for teaching me how to forgive from the heart.

This church had a high value for prayer. The senior pastor's wife led the daytime prayer group, which met in their home. I didn't need to go to work, so I joined the group and learned to pray and intercede. This was around the time when David Yonggi Cho's book, *The Fourth Dimension*, came out. It was filled with his teaching about faith and prayer, which impacted many nations. In those days, we sang the Scripture in song, making many declarations. We sang choruses like, "I am a new creation, I am a brand new man, all things have passed away, I am born again. More than a conqueror, that's who I am. I am a new creation, I am a brand new man." When you sing and focus on these words, you will believe them and become what you believe yourself to be.

The amazing thing is that the pastor was an Australian from Perth. My friends and mine were the only two non-white families in the church. We didn't know it at the time, but this was God's way of preparing us for Australia.

*Unbelievable Miracles, Healing, and Deliverances*

During my time in the Assembly of God church, my heart was stirred up to see people healed. I once saw a woman brought in who was skin and bones because of cancer. The doctors had given up on her and sent her home to die. Her family brought her to church on a stretcher from the hospital, believing for her to be healed. She was laid at the front in the church service. While we were worshipping, she got up and sat beside me. I had my eyes closed, and didn't notice her right away. I thought the chair next to me was empty because my friend was up on the platform in the worship team, but eventually I sensed someone there. When I opened my eyes to see who it was, I was shocked to see this miracle. The whole church went wild in worship and other miracles started to happen. In this church there was a big corner full of wheelchairs, walking sticks, crutches, bottles of pills, packets of cigarettes and lighters, from people who had been healed of their addictions and illnesses.

If you got to the church right at the time the service began, you would have to stand for hours because you could not get a seat. One Sunday morning, the pastor suddenly stopped the worship and called out into the congregation to the lady standing in front of me with a hunchback, and said to her, "To the lady in a green top, the Lord is healing you right now." I watched the hump on her back disappear into her, and she stood straight like nothing had ever happened to her.

I saw legs and arms grow out where there had been only stumps. What an amazing God we serve! I witnessed hundreds of other miracles, which would fill several more pages of this book. All of this inspired me to want to step out in faith and see God move through my own life too.

I decided that I was going to stand up and be counted, and recognize that I am a daughter of the King. I decided that I was not going to allow my past, my failures, my fears, rejection, or shame determine my future and where I was going. There are seeds of greatness in me, I am called to be a deliverer, a princess, to occupy until He comes. I am called to reign in life and set captives free and release the Kingdom of God wherever I go. I came out of hiding, like Gideon, to walk on the call and dreams that are on my life without striving. I have learnt when life gives me lemons I just keep making lemonade out of them and not allow my past to dictate my future. My past have been washed away by the blood of Jesus and made white as snow. I know my Dad loves me and He knows me by name. There are seeds of greatness in me. I am a conqueror. I am victorious. I can do all things through Christ who strengthens me. When you know that you are loved, you feel secure. I know He loves me and this love lifts me up above the waves. I don't need to be overwhelmed. He raises me and put my feet upon the rock so I can stand on solid ground. His mercies are new every morning, every moment, every day and always. This love fills me with joy. I don't need to be afraid anymore. This love will ruin every fear. There is no fear that this love cannot break. It can open every door. 1 will never walk alone. This love lifts me up and I can run fast. He wants me to be me. Anything that would try to disqualify me, "He says, "I am He who blots out your transgressions for My own sake. And I will not remember your sins"(Isaiah 43: 25), Your sins shall be sought but there shall not be found. I will pardon those who I preserve (Jeremiah 50: 20)." All I want to do is to delight God's heart and bring Him glory. I am so grateful for what He has done for me. I will forever praise Him.

# CHAPTER 6

# PASSION FOR THE LOST AND COMPASSION FOR THE SICK AWAKENED

Witnessing the miracles happening around me in my church awakened in me the desire to be used by God. The compassion to see people saved and healed had become stronger than my fear of failure. My first miracle took place at a bus stop in a city called Salisbury, now known as Harare. I had been to the city to do some shopping. When I got to the bus stop, there was a lady sitting there who was in terrible pain to the point of tears. Her leg was so bent that it almost doubled, making it terribly painful and difficult to walk. I remember her telling me that she had had that pain for years and it was getting worse. She had gone to the doctor, but he had given her no hope. My heart was moved with compassion and I asked her, "Can I pray for you?" She said, "Yes, please, if it will help." I asked her, "Can I put my hands on your leg and pray?" She said, "Yes, you can." I put my hand on her knee and commanded the leg to straighten out, the pain to leave, and the leg to be healed in the name of Jesus! To my surprise, the leg shot out and started shaking as the pain was leaving. She grabbed me and kissed me again and again, thanking me. I told her that I had no power to heal, but that it was Jesus who had healed her through me. I then asked her if she would like to receive Jesus into her heart to be her Lord and Savior. She said, "Yes, please." I then led her through the prayer of repentance, and just like that, she was gloriously saved.

I then asked her if she would like me to visit her home to see how she was doing and if she would like to come to church with me. She said, "Yes, please come and pray for my husband too. He has a terrible cough from smoking and he can't stop. He has been smoking for over 40 years." We set a time to meet and I went to their house, where I met her husband. I prayed for him and, to my surprise again, his cough stopped and he gave up smoking. The following Sunday, we went to church and at the end of the service he also gave his heart to the Lord. I was so fired up that I couldn't wait to do it again and again, and I have never stopped. I try and lead people to the Lord wherever I find them, whether on buses, trains, or planes. I especially love ministering to people on the planes because they can't get up and leave. Rather than forcing it on them, I try to get to know them and weave in the gospel in my conversation. I find when I make friends with them first, I have a better chance of them listening to me. It gives me an opportunity to gauge where they are in relation to the Lord and whether or not they are interested in hearing more.

I do this because I have realized that Jesus and the Father don't want to be in heaven without us. It's not God's will that any should perish. For God so loved the world that He gave His only begotten Son, that whoever believes in Him should not perish but have everlasting life. God did not send His Son into the world to condemn the world, but that the world through Him might be saved (John 3:16-17). The Father sent His Son Jesus for the sake of us, His Bride, whom He died for, in order to give us the ministry of reconciliation and so that we might disciple nations back to Jesus. He has also equipped us by sending us the Holy Spirit, who testifies about Jesus.

I just want to stop for a minute or two and encourage you to think about what you have just read. If you have never asked Jesus to come into your heart and be your Lord and Savior, now is the time. I encourage you to stop for a minute and talk to Him. He is waiting for you and will respond to your call. He loves you more than anyone can ever love you. He has a purpose and a plan for your life. If you call on Him, He will come running with open arms. I have seen many lives changed by the love of God; He is the only one who can give true peace that the world can't give nor take away.

# CHAPTER 7

# WITH GOD
# ALL THINGS ARE POSSIBLE

Our country had been experiencing war for some time but in 1979, my husband Bob and I could see that it was not going to be a safe place for bringing up our children. Also, as the hostility grew more intense toward white people, we realized that my husband (who is white) would not be safe there for much longer.

Many people were leaving the country at this time. We had friends whose two sons had migrated to Australia. They went to visit their sons for the holidays and ended up spending a year there. When they came back, they told us about how wonderful the weather was in Australia and how it was a nice place to live. So my husband and I began to pray. Leaving Zimbabwe would not be easy; in an effort to keep people from leaving, the government had passed a law that those who left were only allowed to take $1,000 with them. This did not seem like it would be enough, but we had received peace about our decision to leave. And so, we started our journey of faith. We sold our beautiful home, booked our tickets, gave away everything that we owned, and only packed what we were allowed to take on the plane: four cases of clothes and $1,000.

As difficult as it was to make these sacrifices, I couldn't help but feel a sense of anticipation. I had forgotten about my childhood dreams and desires about all of the countries that I wanted to see. I had learned about Australia and England in school in my geography class when I was young and had always had a desire to go there and see how people lived. At the time it seemed impossible, which is why I am so glad that God is not limited by our circumstances. He looks inside us and gives us the desires of our hearts. At the writing of this book, I have lived in Australia for 37 years and have been to 31 countries. Don't you love the way that God works? He never ceases to surprise me. Truly His ways are beyond our understanding.

### God's Favor and Provision

Our last Sunday night in our church, they prayed and sang over us the chorus "Jehovah-Jireh, my provider, Your grace is sufficient for me." According to the book of Genesis in the Bible, Jehovah-Jireh means "Israel's covenant-keeping God will provide." We soon were to learn just how faithful He is to keep His promises.

The day we arrived in Sydney, Australia, we booked a hotel for one night, put our luggage in the room, and bought a newspaper. We found a park, sat down, and began looking for a job and a house. Not long after, we found a potential job for my husband and an ad for a suitable house. Bob called about the job, was interviewed over the phone, and was asked to start the next day. Afterward, we called about the house and went to see it. It was a furnished duplex with everything we needed. We agreed to rent the house that day and moved in the next. So we only stayed in the hotel one night. Within the first 24 hours of our new life in Australia, the Lord had provided us with a job and a house, and He had only just begun to show us how much He had blessed us.

Before we left Zimbabwe, we purchased tickets for our family to visit New Zealand a month after our move to Australia. We knew that it might be sometime before we would be able to go on a holiday together and wanted to take advantage of the opportunity before we lost it. Bob had told his new boss about this when he was hired. To our surprise, the day before we left, his boss paid him $400 of holiday pay. That is unheard of in Australia! Employees typically work for six months before receiving any holiday pay, and even then it's not much.

God also had given us favor with the family next door. When we first moved into the house, our neighbor "Wolf" (his nickname) said we would not need to buy bread, vegetables, and fruits; he was going to supply it all for us. All we needed to buy was meat and milk. We did not have a car at that time, so my husband took the nearby train to work. Wolf offered his car to us whenever we needed to go somewhere, which allowed us to go to church and go shopping. Wolf used to go to auctions and buy cars, fix them up, and sell them. The day before we left to go to New Zealand, he had been to the auctions, bought a car, and sold it to a young man. While the young man was still there, Wolf came and knocked on our door. He invited me to come see the car, so I followed him outside. He asked me if I liked it. I said, "Yes, I like it. It's very nice." He said, "Go and call your husband." As I brought Bob outside, Wolf asked him, "Do you like this car?" Bob said that he did like the car and was then invited by Wolf to get into the driver's seat and drive it around. My husband turned and said to me, "Get in the back seat, let's go for a drive." As we rode in the car, Wolf said to Bob, "She likes it." Bob said, "It's a nice car, but we have no money to buy it."

When we returned, my husband went back in the house. I said to Wolf, "The car is very nice, but we can't afford it." He said to me, "It's Thursday, I know your husband got paid today." I said, "Yes, but we are going to New Zealand tomorrow. Even if we could afford it, we have nowhere to keep it while we are gone." He then turned to the young man and said, "She likes it. Let her have it; I will give you your money back and get you another one." He had sold the car to the young man for $6,000, but it was worth more than that. It was only five years old and had very little mileage on it. He asked me, "How much can you give me?" I said, "Wolf, I can only afford $300." He said, "Go and get it now, before I change my mind, and I will keep the car in my garage until you come back."

I ran back in the house and said to my husband, "He said he would give us the car for $300!" We were able to pay him with the holiday bonus that Bob had been given, trading one blessing for another. Praise Jesus! The next day, Wolf put our new car into his garage and drove us to the airport. He even came and picked us up upon our return. We were so well looked after; the Lord does not miss a thing.

It truly is amazing what Wolf did for us. He was not very gentlemanly like by any means. He was not very clean, so his wife used to have to steal his clothes to wash them when he went to bed. People used to cross to the other side of the road rather than pass his house. But to us, he was so very kind and gentle. How the Lord led him to do all that he did for us, I will never know. But it just shows me that God can use whomever He chooses to help His children.

One day as he stood in our doorway, Wolf said to my husband, "I have been wondering about what is causing me to do what I am doing for you guys. Then today, I saw your wife's Bible on the table and I knew that was what it is. There is something about your wife that has been causing me to do all this. It's not about you [Bob], but there is something about her and I know it has something to do with her Bible."

We stayed in that house until we could afford to move to a better apartment. We went back six months later to visit and give Wolf and his family gifts to show our gratitude. But they were gone and nowhere to be found. We never saw them again. Sometimes I have wondered if this man had been an angel sent to look after us until we could stand on our feet. We have such an amazing Father; it would not surprise me!

# CHAPTER 8

# FINDING A CHURCH

When we lived in Zimbabwe, we had attended a Pentecostal church, but there weren't any Pentecostal churches near us in Australia; only the more traditional denominations. That was the thing I missed more than anything else: being in corporate, anointed worship where I could experience the tangible presence of God. Once you have tasted the goodness of God, nothing else can ever fulfill or satisfy that hunger. Not having that available to me was extremely difficult, so we decided that we would try to find a church to attend that was more like the one we left in Zimbabwe.

We kept looking until early one Sunday morning we found an Assemblies of God advertisement at the bottom of a newspaper. We called to get their address, which was 25 minutes away from us, and attended that morning's service. The pastor had been there only a year, so it was a small congregation, but he was hungry to see God move, so we decided to make this our home church. It was so wonderful to once again be part of a church where we were invited into the presence of God! One night during a prayer meeting, I was overcome by an uncontrollable joy. I was trying hard to hold it in, not wanting to interrupt the meeting, but when the pastor noticed what was happening to me, he said, "Deborah, let it go. It's the joy of the Lord." When he said that, I allowed the joy in me to break out and spread across everyone there. From that night on, more people started coming to the prayer meetings; they didn't want to miss out on what God was doing. One night, a lady came she was manifesting in a deep, manly voice. She was delivered that night and became a faithful follower of the Lord. She never missed a prayer night meeting from that point on. She even started bringing her husband and children along, all of who were eventually saved. Day by day, the Lord added to our numbers.

*An Encounter with the Father*

The church had a women's camp in our first year there. I was very blessed. Then when we went the following year. I said to the Lord, " This time I don't want just to be blessed. I also want to be a blessing."

During worship in the first session of the camp, I had an encounter with the Father. He took me back to when I was a toddler. He was sitting on a huge rock and I was sitting on His lap. There was clear water gushing out of the rock underneath Him. He said, "Baby drink as much as you want. You will never thirst again and you will never have to go to the well to carry a heavy bucket again." I was so happy as He rocked me back and forth on His big lap. When I came out of that encounter, I knew I had been healed of the pain of going to carry water with a big bucket when I was young.

After the session, we went to have supper in the dining room. As I sat down, the Lord said to me, "You remember that you said, "You want to be a blessing and not just receive in this camp?" I said, " Yes Lord." He said, "You see that lady sitting at the other table facing you. I want you to give her four hundred dollars." Wanting to please the Lord even though not knowing how I was going to do it, I said, "Lord I am willing but You know we don't have the money.

But if You give it to me, I will give her. Lord I trust You to provide it without me asking my husband for it."

When I first started working, I signed at TAFE COLLEGE to learn fashion. So after class, I didn't have a sewing machine to practice on what I had learnt. There was a man who came to our house selling sewing machines. But it was different to what they had at TAFE. I didn't like it. My husband bought it anyway. But one day I was looking in the newspaper and there was a machine like the ones at TAFE. My husband said, "Call and find out if it's still there and go and buy it. I did, and it was still there. I went and bought it. I was happy. It was still very new and the lady asked for half of the price she paid. It had been only used twice and the daughter had changed her mind about sewing at school.

Without me saying a word to my husband about the four hundred dollars, He said to me, "You have that sewing machine in the cupboard, why don't you get rid of it. I don't care what you do with the money. Just get rid of it. It's wasting space." I went to work that night. My work colleague said to me, " Deborah I remember you bought a sewing machine you never used. My friend has started learning to sew. I told her about your sewing machine. She gave me four hundred dollars for it. Can you bring it tomorrow, here is the money?" I said, "She paid for the machine without seeing it?" She said, "Yes I told her that I trust you, and the machine is still new in the box. So here is the money bring it tomorrow."

So the following Sunday, I was able to give the lady the four hundred dollars after the morning service. When I went to the evening service, she grabbed me by the hand and said, "Come outside." I went with her to the car park. She said, "Look what your money has done. I was short of four hundred dollars to get this car to drive my children to school before I go to work." She was a single mum. We hugged and thanked the Lord for what He had done. I was so grateful for the opportunity the Lord had given me to be a blessing to her. I was also glad that I had obeyed the Lord not knowing how the money was going to come. Truly it's a greater joy to give than to receive (Act 20:35).

# UNDER HIS WINGS

## *Promotion Comes from the Lord*

After our first year in Australia, I decided to go to work. I had not worked for years because we were financially comfortable in Zimbabwe, but now we needed to have two incomes in order to save enough to put down a house deposit. There was a level of racism in Australia at that time against dark-skinned people, aboriginal and foreigners alike, but I had no trouble finding work; I had very good references.

I found a nursing job in a hospital. This meant that I would have to miss attending church on a regular basis, but it was a sacrifice that I chose to make. The Lord had blessed me with very good skills and I did well in my role, so much so that I was soon asked to begin training the new hires. Unfortunately, when some of the members of staff saw that I had favor with the boss, they became jealous. Many of them were racist, which was already making it difficult for me at work. They began changing the roster so that I was constantly paired with employees who were lazy, which made me have to work even harder.

Even though I struggled with my frustration, I never complained to the boss about what was happening. Instead, I kept taking it to the Lord in prayer. I think that it irritated some of the nurses that they couldn't annoy me enough to complain about them. One day, at 6:00 in the morning in the middle of winter, I was in the shower helping a patient. One of the nurses came into the shower, turned the water from hot to cold, put it to full blast, and directed it right at me. I was soaked to the bone, shoes and all. She looked at me, waiting for my response. I just looked at her and said, "I am wet." She stomped out, furious that I was not upset enough to fight her. Shortly after, my partner who was a very nice nurse walked in and found me all wet. She asked me, "Did this patient do that to you?" I told her who had done it and she asked me, "What did you do about it?" When I told her that I had done nothing, she became angry with me and said, "If you don't do something about it, I will." She waited all day, but I did not go and complain to the director of nursing. So, before our shift was over, she reported the nurse to our boss. The director waited for me to go to her and report my coworker, though I never did. I chose instead to voice my complaint to the Lord. Two weeks after this incident, my family and I were watching the news on TV when a story came on featuring the very same nurse who had sprayed me with the water. She had been exposed for simultaneously working and getting unemployment benefits. She never returned to the hospital after that. When we trust the Lord to vindicate us, He surely does a better job than a boss.

Although that nurse had left the hospital, I was still treated unfairly by a number of my co-workers. A month later, our boss called me into the office and told me that they were aware of what was going on. They were very happy with my work and didn't want me to leave. So they created a new position for me in the same department but would allow me to not have to work with the nurses who had been unkind to me. It made them quite angry because they had been working there longer than I had. They grumbled, but I didn't say a word. When the boss heard about their complaints, she just told me that if anyone gave me grief about the new position, I was to tell them to go and see management about it. One of the benefits of this new position was that it allowed me to choose which days and shifts that I wanted to work. This enabled me to have Sundays off so that I could regularly attend church with my family.

*Obedience saves lives*

One day I came from the hospital after a night shift, after I had my quiet time with the Lord. Then I went to get into bed and the Lord said, "Pray for Shirley." I said, "Lord I am tired." But the Lord said, "Pray for Shirley." The tone of His voice let me know that it was urgent. So I went back on my knees and prayed for her. After praying I called her to see what was going on. When she answered the phone she was gasping for breath and said, " Thank you. Thank you for listening to the Lord! I was being choked. I was given a gift, from the Japanese ship that came into the Sydney harbor by people I baby-sit for, before school and after school. They bought it not knowing that it was demonic. They were not Christians and didn't know that some souvenirs are demonic; they are used in demonic ceremonies. So I told her to take it out of her house and burn it. I had already broken its power to harm her in prayer.

Then another time I came from work and had my time with the Lord. Then when I went to get into bed, the Lord said, " Pray for Colonel Gaddafi." I said, " Lord who wants to pray for Colonel Gaddafi? He does not need praying for, he needs shooting." But the Lord said, " Deborah Pray." So back on my knees I went and prayed. Then I went to bed. I didn't hear anything until six months later. When the Sanford's came to Australia again. Just before he started the first session, he said, " I am going to talk to some people here. You know who you are by what I am going to say, " Six months ago, the Lord told you to pray for Colonel Gaddafi and you said, "Lord who wants to pray for Colonel Gaddafi, he needs shooting?" But in obedience you prayed anyway. The Lord is saying to you, "Thank you for praying. You saved the lives of two hundred people who were on board in the plane Gaddafi was about to shoot down." Then Mr. Sanford said, "I was one of them that also prayed, and I had said the same thing too. I prayed as I was commanded by the Lord." When I heard Mr. Sanford say this, boy was I glad that I had been obedient in praying. That taught me a lesson to pray when God asks me to. It could mean the difference between life and death.

For months the Lord had been giving me dreams about ministry before I knew that I had been called to the field. In my dreams, I would be preaching powerful messages and then would stop and say to myself, "Is all this revelation actually coming out of me?" On the night of December 2, 1981, He encountered me through what I would describe as a dream or a vision wherein I was taken to a huge building. At the entrance were what looked like two cashier's machines, one with a big letter D over it and the other with a B There was a person standing behind each one. As I got closer, wondering which one to go through, the person behind D called out and said, "You come through here." Then the one behind B with a booming voice said, "No, she must not. She comes through here!" All of a sudden I was aware that D stood for "death" and B stood for "born again." So I entered in through B, and as I did so, the atmosphere changed; the feeling was indescribable. The inside of the building was glorious! As I started to walk in, the Lord appeared before me and I fell on my knees. Because of the awesomeness of His presence, I could not lift up my head to look into His face. He called out my name. "Deborah, Deborah, Deborah, follow Me."

He turned and started walking back in the direction from which He had come. I stood up and started following Him. He approached a wall in the building, turned back, and called my name again, "Deborah, Deborah, Deborah, follow Me!" I responded shouting back, "Yes, Lord," with my hands lifted up. Then and there I knew that if I followed Him behind the wall, I was not going to come back. Then the vision ended and I sat up in my bed. I turned to look at my husband, wondering what he thought of me shouting, "Yes, Lord," in the middle of the night. But I was relieved to find out that he was fast asleep and hadn't heard a thing. That vision left a mark on my life. I did not tell a soul for a long time. I just pondered it in my heart.

### Shaking Under the Power of the Holy Spirit

When I did share these dreams with my pastor, he began inviting me to preach on Sunday nights. He specifically encouraged me to preach on what I had preached about in my dreams. Little by little, I gained confidence and courage as he gave me more opportunities to preach. Through these opportunities, I was connected with a godly woman in our church she was a leader in a ministry called Women's Aglow International. One day, my friend invited me to be their guest speaker. This was my first public speaking engagement outside the church. When the day came, I spent time in prayer at home before heading to the meeting. As I prayed, I began to shake under the power of the Holy Spirit. I was used to this during my private prayer time and sometimes in bed, but I was not expecting it to happen that day. The shaking stopped while I was driving to the meeting, but as soon as I stepped into the meeting hall, it started again. I quickly found a seat and sat down. It was in the middle of winter, so when my friend saw the shaking, she thought I was cold. She offered me her jacket to put on my legs to keep warm. I was not cold, but I graciously received it and covered my legs so that the shaking would not be so obvious. When I stood to preach, the shaking stopped until it was time to minister to people. My hand shook when I stretched it out to pray over someone. As soon as my hand was over those whom I prayed for, before I even touched them, their bodies would shake and fall to the floor. When they got up, they were completely healed. I think I was more amazed by what the Lord did that morning than anyone else there. Not long after this, I joined Women's Aglow and helped to start a fellowship and a church, in Sydney, both of which still meet to this day.

*Keeping Focus Opens the Door of Blessing*

In July 1984, we had a national Women's Aglow conference scheduled in Brisbane, the biggest city of the state of Queensland. As I sat in church one Sunday morning my mind wandered off. I started thinking about what I was going to wear at the conference as Aglow women dress well. Then the Lord interrupted my wandering thoughts and said, "Deborah you are busy worrying about what you are going to wear instead of preparing your heart for what you are going there for." I quickly repented and asked Him to help me to be focused on the why. To my surprise at the end of the service one of the young ladies came to me and said, "Deborah, I work for a designer company. We are having a sale party. It is by invitation only and I would love you to come. Here are two tickets, some clothes are ridiculously reduced to make room for the new design." I took my daughter Hazel with me and we bought beautiful outfits that we could not have been able to afford in a million years. When the Lord does things He exceeds our expectation. At the conference people kept asking me, "What does your husband do?" To some I was able to share my testimony.

Prior to coming to this conference, I had been asking the Lord to give me spiritual understanding of some Scriptures in the Old Testament. I continued to pray about this throughout the conference until one night in my hotel, I told the Lord I was not going to bed until He spoke to me. I got the revelation I had been seeking at 1:00 in the morning. I was so excited that I got out of bed, completely forgetting where I was, and started dancing and praising the Lord. The next thing I knew, there was a knock on my door. I opened the door gently and saw that it was my neighbor from across the hall. Realizing the hour, I began to apologize for being so loud, but to my surprise, she came in saying, "Don't be sorry, I want to hear about what you've received." I shared with her what I had received from the Lord. She was excited because she had been asking to have the understanding of the same Scriptures.

This breakthrough increased the hunger that had been growing inside me to know the Word of God more. I knew that one way to grow in my knowledge was to go to Bible school. I was attending a church that had a Bible school, but when enrollment opened up, I was too afraid to register. The next day, the Lord asked me why I didn't enroll in Bible school. I confessed to Him that I didn't think I was capable of doing it. He said to me, "I want you to go and tell the pastor in charge of enrollment why you didn't enroll." The following Sunday, I went to church with the intention of talking with the pastor once the service was over. Right in the middle of his sermon, he suddenly stopped and said, "I feel the Lord has just changed my message." He started talking instead about David in the Bible. As he spoke, the Lord sent me a vision of my childhood, back to the day that my stepmother beat me for something I had not done and I ran into the bush crying and hugged a rock. The Lord said to me, "I was the rock on which you cried and to which you clung. I want you to tell the pastor that I changed his message for you, so that he knows that I want you to enroll. Like David, I took him from the field where he was attending his father's sheep (Psalm 78:70)." In that moment, the love of God enveloped me like a blanket and I started to weep. At the end of the service, I told the pastor all that the Lord had told me. He said, "Deborah, we recognize the anointing of God on your life. Now I want you to enroll and we will do our best to help you with what you need." So I did enroll and completed three years of ministry training. I loved it and I grew in the knowledge of the Word of God.

In order to graduate, it was required of us to go out and do ministry during the last semester of the program. The Lord had given me favor with the hospital chaplain in the hospital I worked. As it turned out, working with the chaplain on my days off would not give me enough ministry hours to graduate, so she offered to introduce me to the pastor who looked after all their campuses. The hospital was part of this ministry. I met the pastor and his wife and began going with them to different branches of the ministry every week. He gave me opportunities to preach in his place, which not only increased my hours but my experience in ministry. The pastor began inviting me to preach on these Sundays, often without notice. I quickly learned how to walk in humility and in complete dependence on the Holy Spirit as I preached His word to many, many people. Soon after, this pastor blessed me with the opportunity of holding my own healing meetings once a week in Sydney in their city campus. God did amazing things; I saw Him heal physical, emotional and spiritual needs. All the while that I attended Bible school I still worked part time at the hospital on the night shift. I slept only three hours a day for three years, which is a miracle in itself. It is amazing what you can manage when you choose to obey the Lord, especially while you are still young.

After graduating from the Bible school, I had a dream I had completed the Teen Challenge program. I was on the streets ministering to drug and alcohol addicts, prostitutes, and the homeless. I told my husband about my dream and that I wanted to receive training to do street ministry. He told me that I could enroll in the program if I wanted to, and so I did. The amazing thing is that the building I had seen in my dream a few years earlier was the same building where the training was held. I worked in King's Cross in Sydney, where I saw many come to the Lord. Several people chose to go to the rehabilitation center and get clean. Some of them even went into ministry themselves. I was still nursing part time and found that the training I received was becoming handy in my work at the mental hospital and would be helpful later on in my ministry journey. God does not waste anything.

While all this was happening, I began to see many come to the Lord in the hospital where I worked as well. One of the nurses with whom I worked the night shift with had an issue of bleeding which would cause her a lot of pain. One night, the compassion of the Lord touched my heart as we were working together. I stopped what I was doing and said to her, "Carmel, will you let me pray for you?" She said, "Yes, please." I prayed for her and then we went back to work. The next day I asked her how she was. She said, "Fine." I left it at that. A month went by, but she hadn't said anything about how she was doing. While attending a conference in another state, the Lord asked me to pray for another friend who was in another country. I said, "Lord, You want me to pray for someone in another country yet You have not healed Carmel. I thought you would heal her so that she would know how much You love her and come to know you as her Lord." The Lord said to me, "Deborah, your business is to pray; healing is My business." I quickly repented and agreed to pray for both of my friends. After I returned from the conference, I went back to work and ran into Carmel. I asked her how she was doing and again she said, "I am fine." I said, "Carmel, you know what I mean." She said, "Deborah, I am so sorry that I have taken so long to tell you. I was healed that night when you prayed for me. The bleeding stopped. But I wanted to wait a month to make sure." Hugging her I said, "Carmel, I am so happy for you. I am also happy that you are sure it's not going to come back." I never preached to her; I just lived my life as I felt called to live it.

One day she came to work and said to me, "Tomorrow, I will not be able to sleep." I said, "Why not?" She said, "My friend had a baby a couple of months ago, but now the older sibling is in hospital dying of asthma." I said to her, "Would you like me to pray for her son? In the Bible, the disciples prayed over handkerchiefs and sent them to the sick so that they would be healed. I can't go to the hospital to pray for him, so I will pray over a handkerchief and put it in an envelope. Tomorrow, give it to your friend to take to the hospital and tell her to put it on her boy and say, 'Receive healing from Deborah's God.'" The next day, she and her friend followed my instructions and instantly the boy was healed. During the doctor's morning rounds, the boy was up and running around. The doctors said to the mother, "Your boy does not need to be here. You can take him home." She took him home that day and that boy never had another attack again. The Lord began to radically change Carmel's life. She had been living with a man at the time, but the Lord encouraged them both through separate people to live separately until they were married. Not long after they both gave their hearts to the Lord and were baptized. Following this act of faith, they were married. This was just one of the testimonies wherein the Lord showed me just how strong the power of prayer really is. Allow me to share a few more with you!

One morning, I was working in another section when one of the nurses came to me with tears in her eyes and said, "Deborah, can you please pray for me? I have come from the doctor and he told me that I have cancer on my nose and ear. He said I have to have an operation to cut out the cancer." I said, "I will come to pray with you at the morning tea break," which was in only 15 minutes away. All

I could think was how terrible it would be for her to have her nose cut off. The ear can be covered with hair, but what can you do for the nose? I went and prayed for her. The next day she went back to the doctor and they could not find the cancer. Praise the wonderful name of Jesus.

There was a lady who worked in the kitchen who was expecting a child. She and her husband had waited a long time to get pregnant, but when she went to the doctor she was given a bad report. She was told that her baby had Down's syndrome and that she should abort the baby. Although she was not a believer, when she had heard the testimony of the nurse whom the Lord had healed of the cancer on the nose, she came to me, crying and asking for prayer. I prayed for her baby to be healthy and normal. I did not give her any advice as to what decision to make, even though she asked me, "What would you do if you were in my shoes?" I said, "I cannot give an answer. But we can pray, and I will continue to pray for you and your husband." I did continue to pray for them. One day she came and told me that they had decided to keep the baby. She said, "What if they are wrong?" I told her that we must trust the Lord, but she said, "I don't know Him." I said, "Would you like to know Him?" She said that she would and I was able to lead her to the Lord. I continued to pray for them until the baby was born. I am glad to tell you that he was a healthy baby boy. I love it when the Lord does the unexpected, especially when the doctors have no explanation for it.

Another time, while I was still working morning shift, I was blessed to help care for a lady who'd been diagnosed with dementia. Her friends who used to visit her told me her story. She'd been a lovely Christian lady before her illness, but she had become quite confused and could be very aggressive. It was hard to even feed and dress her. One morning, I went to help her get into the shower and found that her countenance had changed and that she was in her right mind. She lifted her head from the pillow to wish me a good morning, smiled, and said, "I am going to die today." I knew it was true; she had never been able to say a full sentence when she came

59

to us. It was so good for me to see that she had been restored before she died. The dementia no longer had any power over her. I ran to the office and asked my supervisor to call her family to see that their mother had been restored before she died. Her two daughters and their husbands came in shortly after. They were so grateful that I had done that for them. I went in to give her morning tea at 10:00 AM. She looked at each one of her daughters and sons-in-law and smiled at them. She took one more sip of tea, smiled, and said, "Thank you, that will do." I left the room to give the family time alone with her. Peacefully, she went to be with Lord at 11:00 AM.

I wish I could tell you the same good news about my next patient. Oh, how I wished she had had the same experience as the other lady. I am sorry to tell you the sad story of what bitterness can do to a person.

There was a woman who was a wife of a Uniting Church pastor being treated in our hospital. At her time of death, she was so scared to die. She was screaming with terror. Her face looked shocked, like she was seeing a ghost. I asked her, "Why you are so afraid?" She said, "I am scared to die because they are coming for me. They are so scary." I said, "Why are they coming for you?" She said, "Because I will not forgive my husband for what he did to me." I said, "Can I pray for you, for God to help you forgive him?" She said, "No, I will never forgive him for what he did to me." I said, "Please forgive him. Whatever he did, can it be compared with what you are going through now?" She screamed again, with her fingers curled in like when a person with demons manifests, and shouted, "I will never forgive him!" Her face turned blue like a reptile. I tried desperately to help her to forgive, but she would not. She died a horrible death alone with her husband sitting outside her ward in the corridor. Holding onto bitterness and not forgiving her husband had robbed her of the peace that only comes from the Lord.

I remember my own experience, when I was in Bible school. I had an assignment of twelve hundred words on "What is new under the sun (Ecclesiastes 1:9)? A friend invited me to her house for morning tea. I said, "I am sorry, I can't come. I have an assignment to do and I don't know where to start." After sitting for a while not knowing what to do. I thought I might as well go and have morning tea with my friend. So I rang her back and went to her house. When I got there, I found she had also invited a couple who were mutual friends from church. We had a nice time catching up. I did not talk about my assignment at all. As I was leaving at the door, I put my arms around my friend hugging her and said, "Thank you for having me. I am glad I came. Now I better go and work on my assignment." While she was still in my arms, she said something that cut me like a scissors, "I know why you came here. You came to pick these people's brains for your assignment." There and then I had a decision to make, what to do with my pain. Whilst I still had her in my arms I said, "Dad I give You my pain. I give you my pain, devil I know it's you and I know that my friend loves me. She would never hurt me intentionally." I kissed my friend and left. The pain was still there. As I drove home, I kept repeating, "Dad I give You my pain, I know my friend loves me and would never hurt me intentionally. Devil I know it's you." I kept it up until the pain left. It left before I got home. Then I said, "Dad please give me what to write on my assignment. You know what is new under the sun." By the time I got home I knew what to write. Miraculously I was able to write my assignment. I had victory.

That day I was going to work night shift. That evening the same friend fell and broke her collarbone. Before she went unconscious, she told her husband to call me and ask for pray and to go and visit her in the hospital. When I got home from work, there was a message on my answering machine. I was glad that I had not taken offence. I would not have been able to pray effectively or visit her in hospital.

She was in a four bed ward. I drew the curtains around her and prayed. When I finished praying, I drew back the curtains. The three ladies in the ward with her asked me if I could pray for them. I did and ended up leading two of them to the Lord. How I was glad that I had not taken offence, I would have missed out on the opportunity of winning souls.

How wonderful it is if we can deal with the pain of offence without the other person ever knowing that the enemy used them to hurt us. How many relationships would be spared the pain of broken relationships? Just doing what I have just shared has helped me tremendously and I have been able to help others do the same. I just want to encourage you as you read this. If someone has hurt you, please choose to forgive them, even if you don't feel like you can; forgiveness is a decision, not a feeling. Forgiving someone doesn't mean that what they did was right. But it will set you free and God will heal your pain and give you a brand new start. He heals broken hearts and binds up their wounds (Psalm 147: 3).

# CHAPTER 9

# PERSECUTION STARTED

After I finished Bible school, I was offered a better job at a private psychiatric hospital. When God puts His favor on you, it follows you wherever you go. But don't forget that with favor also comes persecution, like Joseph who had favor with his father Jacob, but was hated by his brothers.

My new job was supposed to be in a "Christian" hospital, but it was Christian by name only. I used to come to work early so that I could pray and ask the Lord to shift the environment, bringing His presence into the hospital. When people started to get healed and delivered, I began to be called into the director of nursing's office. Apparently, the doctors had been complaining that I was not employed as a chaplain and that I should not pray for patients; if I continued there would be problems. But I never went to any patient and asked them if I could pray for them or if they would like to receive Jesus as their Lord and Savior. The patients themselves noticed that there was something different about me. They would ask me to pray that they would receive the same peace that I carried within me. I saw many patients come to the Lord and be delivered and healed.

Some of these patients who had been seeing psychiatrists for several years were now telling the doctors that they did not need their pills anymore. When the doctors heard this from their patients, they were not very happy with me because they were now losing business. It was a similar situation to the one in the book of Acts 16:16-24, when the slave girl who had been able to predict the future due to demonic possession was delivered and her masters started losing profit.

The hospital's management team seemed to be looking for a way to fire me, so while I was on my day off, they called a mandatory staff meeting knowing full well that I was the only one who wouldn't be there. They told the rest of the staff that it was imperative to be there and not to talk about it to whoever was not there. When I came back to work, everyone was asking, "Where were you? We had a meeting yesterday, and the director of nursing said, 'Whoever was not there must go and see him in his office.'"

The last blow was when a patient who had worked in an abortion clinic was being treated in my section of the hospital. She was screaming so much, saying, "I don't want to kill my baby." Even though they had given her medication, it made no difference. The doctors had planned to send her to a public psychiatric hospital that was better equipped to handle unmanageable patients than we were. When I came on duty, I went to her ward to see my supervisor who was assisting the doctor. As I was going to leave the room, she screamed saying, "Please, Deborah, don't leave the room! You are the only one the devil fears. When you walked in, he went and stood in the corner." So I quietly bound the devil, and she stopped manifesting. I told the two doctors and my supervisor, "I think she is going to be okay now. She does not need to go to the other hospital." I was trying to save them from the embarrassment of sending a patient that did not need to be treated. But they said to me, "Pack her bag, she is going." So she went to the public hospital, they looked at her and sent her back, saying that she did not need to be locked up or medicated. Our doctors were rather embarrassed when the ambulance brought her back. A few days later, the patient said that she was feeling better and wanted to go home. It was a voluntary hospital, so they had to let her go. After this, it became quite difficult to work there, as I was being watched all the time. I continued to rely on the Lord for courage and wisdom, not knowing then just how much I was going to need Him in the years to come.

CHAPTER 10

# DRINKING FROM THE CUP OF SUFFERING: PAYING THE PRICE

The Lord had asked me to pray in the church from 6:00-7:00 AM every day except Sunday for 18 months. The pastor gave me a key to the church so I could come and go as I needed. Before the 18 months were up, we outgrew the church building. By then God had blessed my husband and I immensely. We had two houses and a prosperous construction business, so Bob offered to extend the church building at our cost. But on the day that he was doing the last touches on the church building before the opening day, something was said to him that cut him to the heart. He came home extremely upset and said to me, "Never ask me to go to that church again!" He never told me what was said or done to him. Up to this day I don't know what happened to him. Maybe the Lord in His wisdom protected me, knowing that I will have enough to handle without having to deal with forgiving the people that had hurt him and destroyed my marriage. Even though I don't understand it, I praise and thank Him because He knows best.

Two days later, Bob said to me, "Now you have a decision to make: it's God or our marriage. You cannot have both. I am giving you three years to choose." The next day I went to a Women's Aglow meeting. The guest speaker was Jackie Pullinger, a missionary from Hong Kong. God could not have used a better person to encourage me than a woman who had known how to trust the Lord in the midst of opposition. She started by sharing her testimony and then went on to her message. Then she stopped and said, "The Lord has just changed my message. There is someone here that the Lord wants me to speak to." She took out her Bible and read from Isaiah 41:7-14. In seven verses the Lord speaks the following to His people: "Fear not, for I am with you, I am Your God. Fear not, I will help you. I will hold your right hand, saying to you, 'Fear not, I will help you.' Fear not, I will help you, says the Lord, Your Redeemer, the Holy One of Israel." When she read that, I felt the love of the Father enveloping me like a warm blanket. She stopped for a while, letting me soak in it, before continuing on with her message.

I have learned that when the Lord repeats something, He really wanted me to get it because I was going to need it. He wanted me to know that even though the journey of faith on which I was about to embark was not going to be an easy road, He was going to be with me all the way. I can truly say, "He has been faithful in the wind and in the storm. In the wind and in the rain, He has been faithful."

The next three years were very difficult years in our marriage, as my husband stopped going to church. He didn't want anything to do with our friends from church, even our good friends whom we used to do everything with, whom we used go on holidays with, and whose children our children used to play with. Coincidentally, it was also the time when church leaders were falling. That didn't help my situation at all; my faith was sorely tested. I continued to do what any married woman would do for her husband in her home, but what do you do when a man is comparing himself with God? I knew he was angry with the Lord. He had been an adopted child, but lost both his adopted parents by the time he was 21. Now he had been hurt in the church, a place where he thought he should have been healed. I think that he felt forsaken by God. If I had known what I know now, I would have been able to help him. He would have been healed of the orphan spirit.

Three months before the end of the three years that Bob had given me to choose God or marriage, the Lord gave me five clear dreams at different times, which I still remember to this day:

**The first dream:** I was walking through a path and the sick were laid out on each side of the street. As I walked, I stretched out my hands and said, "Be healed in Jesus' name," and people would get up healed. I did not stop to check how they were because I knew that they were healed. Then I came to a roundabout and saw that there was a man mocking things of God, like in the book of Acts 13:6-11. I pointed at him and said, "You shall be blind." Immediately the man went blind. He begged me to pray for him that he might see. I did and he was able to see again. Then I continued to walk and pray for the sick, and they were all healed.

**The second dream:** I was walking in a path like the first dream. There were white houses all along the streets, like in the Greek islands. But just before I got to the roundabout, I knew that one of the houses up on the left side was mine. I walked up to it and saw that the door was open. Inside were boxes everywhere, all beautifully wrapped up with big ribbons and bows like wedding presents. Some had been opened already and some had not. In the dream I realized that they were all my spiritual gifts, and that I would open the rest later.

**The third dream:** I was walking along a path similar to the ones before, but this one was longer and there was no one else around; there were only shrubs scattered about on each side of the path. The ground was flat and the air was calm and clear, allowing me to see far in every direction. There was one bush that was taller than the others and closer to the path. It had dainty leaves, like those from a jacaranda. As I was walking I thought about how my husband was not with me. I turned and saw the Lord standing by the shrub that had stood out from the rest. There was a delicate branch over His face as He watched me walk. I really wanted to say, "Lord, please remove the branch from Your face so I can see You." But the awesomeness of His presence left me speechless. I said to myself, "The fact that You are here watching me makes me grateful." So I continued to walk as He watched me. I walked as far as the eye could see and all the while, the Lord continued to watch after me. I kept turning to look at Him until I was so far away that I couldn't see Him anymore.

**The fourth dream:** I had a repeat of the third dream.

**The fifth dream:** Again I had a repeat of the third dream, but this time several people came and were attacking me. I was given a rod like Moses' but it was so tall and heavy that I could not lift it up. Instead I swayed it back and forth. When I touched an enemy with it, the enemy would die and its body would disintegrate. But they kept coming from out of nowhere. I cried to the Lord saying, "Oh Lord! They are too many!" I looked around and saw a whole other army approaching. But suddenly I realized that the second group was for me; they took over and won the battle. After they triumphed, I again reflected on how my husband was not with me.

From that time on, I knew that I was going to be on this journey alone, without Bob. But the Lord was going to be with me. My heart was settled on my decision to go with the Lord. It was not easy, but I knew there was no plan B. I had prayed and prayed for my marriage to stand, but what I had hoped for did not come to be. I chose to have an inheritance, incorruptible and undefiled, that does not fade away and is reserved in heaven for me.

Shortly after the last dream, my husband came home after work and said, "Three years is up and it looks like God has won, so I am leaving." He went into the bedroom and packed his suitcase. As he headed to the door, he said to me, "I want everything sold: the houses, furniture, all we own." Then he left.

The next day when I went to work, I was told that the management had decided to cut down on staff, and that I was going to be the first to go. I told my boss what David said in Psalm 37: "I was young and now I am old, yet I have never seen the righteous forsaken nor their children begging bread" (Psalm 37:25). As I left that office, I felt like the rug had been pulled out from under me, and that there was a gaping hole in front of me into which I was about to fall. I decided then and there that if I entertained that thought, I would surely be defeated. So, instead, I decided to call on God. I found a quiet place and poured out my heart to Him. I said, "Holy Spirit, You were sent to be the Comforter. I need You now! You are my strength in my weakness. You light up my darkness. I need You to wrap me in Your loving arms." I cried my heart out. After I pulled myself together, I went back to the nurses' station. My supervisor took one look at me and said to me, "What is wrong, Deborah? I have never seen you like this before. You are the sunshine in this place. Tell me what's happened." I told her what I had just been told by the boss and that my husband left last night after giving me a choice between God or marriage. She said, "Now I know why the Lord told me to put this book in my bag. I read it when I was deserted as a missionary in France without any money. Take it to a quiet place and read it." The book was called, My Hiding Place by Corrie Ten Boom. As I read through a couple of pages, I found the comfort to carry me through the day until I got home.

When I got home, I let it all out to the Lord. I cried myself to sleep. I woke up with my eyes swollen and no voice, having lost it in all the crying. I looked at myself in the mirror and said to myself, "Deborah, that is not a face of a winner! Devil, you want a fight? You've got one. One of us is going to lose and it's not going to be me!" I hopped in the shower, got dressed, and put makeup on. I burst through my front door and marched around my house seven times, all the while worshiping, just as the Lord had commanded Joshua to do at Jericho. I was shouting at the top of my lungs even though I had no voice. By the sixth or seventh time, my voice was back. I went back into the house and was ready to pray. I knelt in my place of prayer and got lost in prayer until I fell asleep. I know that the battle was won that day, even though nothing had changed in the natural. There was no food in the house because my husband was supposed to go shopping the next day while I was at work. There was no money in the house either, so I decided to go to the bank the next day to withdraw money to buy food. But when I got there, the bank teller told me that Bob had taken out all the money and closed the account. It was so embarrassing because all the tellers knew me, as this was where we had kept our business account. I went to that bank every week to draw money for the wages of the people that worked for us.

I returned home and called on the Holy Spirit to comfort me and to tell me what to do. I waited for Him to answer. I chose not to call my pastor or friends. Instead I embraced failure and learned to deal with the disappointment I felt. I had to keep renewing my mind and choose not to allow my mind to focus on the problems circling around me, attempting to gain mastery. When I went to bed that night, my spiritual eyes were suddenly opened and I could see a thick dark cloud like smoke approaching the front door. Somehow I knew it was a spirit of death coming to kill me. As it came into the room, there was a chilling feeling. It looked like there were gremlins in the room, taunting me and saying, "We are going to kill you tonight and no one will ever know." As the cloud approached, I felt this cold, deathly feeling creeping upon my body, up to my chest. I prayed, but nothing was happening. I said, "Lord, if you don't do something, people will just think I died of a heart attack." Then the Lord said, "Rebuke it and speak the blood." I did and within seconds, it was gone.

I learned something that night. The Lord has given us the

authority to overcome the enemy by the blood of Jesus; He is not going to do it for us. We have to apply the blood and speak out, just as Revelation 12:11 says: "We overcome the enemy by the blood of the Lamb and the word of our testimony." I am convinced that if I had just lain there waiting for the Lord to do it, I wouldn't be writing about it today. So I renewed my mind to be more focused on His presence in my life and spirit. When I seek His face and speak to Him, He opens my mind and equips me for the strenuous climb ahead. I have chosen to walk by faith and not by sight, trusting Him to open up the way before me.

The next day I went to the mailbox and found a tiny envelope, just like the olden days' tithing envelopes. I opened it and inside was one hundred and twenty dollars in cash and a little note that said, "The Lord told me to send you cash and not a check because you need the money now." I thanked the Lord and the lady He had used to bless me and then went to the supermarket and bought food.

Two weeks after my husband left, he came home and told me that he was miserable. I said, "If you apologize, you can come back home." He said, "Me, apologize? Never. I want everything sold, the houses and all the furniture." Then he left the house and drove off. When he saw that I was not miserable, he became very bitter and started doing unthinkable things to try and make me unhappy. He would come at night and turn on the outside water tap and leave it running or take fuses out of the meter box. One night when I was out, he brought a gas bottle and opened it outside the front door. I got home, saw the gas bottle, and could smell gas. I was terrified and didn't know what to do, so I called the police. I could not stay inside the house because it was full of gas and I was scared to be outside in the dark. The police came and drove around the streets near my house to let my husband know that they were aware of what he was doing in case he was hanging around. They told me to get a court order to stop him from coming near me. If he did come around, they would have authority to arrest him. The Lord gave me favor with the chamber of magistrate, who gave me the court order on the spot that would stop Bob from harassing me or coming near me.

The following week, sometime in the night, house bills were shoved under my door. I don't know if Bob came himself or sent someone else to the house at night. All the bills had expired, which meant I might get all the services in the house cut off if I didn't pay them soon. I took those bills and laid them before the Lord, like Hezekiah in 2 Kings 19:14. I had a good reason to humble myself before the Lord, as I had no means of paying those bills. Two days later, I received a check for $432 from an insurance company, which was just enough to cover all the bills. I called them and asked them why I had received the check, to which they replied, "We don't know anything about it, but feel free to cash it." I took it to the bank, cashed it, and paid the bills; I even had enough leftover to buy a loaf of bread and a liter of milk. How faithful is our God! He comes to our aid in so many ways.

I knew that I needed a job, but I had told the Lord that I was not going to look for one. I could not bear to face another rejection so soon. So, without my knowing it, the Lord put it on another lady's heart to look for a job for me until she found one. After a month, my phone rang at 7:00 in the morning. When I answered it, this same lady told me that she found a job for me in the paper and gave me the number to call. She told me that it was the Lord that told her to find a job for me and to call me when she found one. I said, "If the Lord told you to do that for me, then I will call them." When I called about the nursing job, I was interviewed right there at home, sitting in my lounge, and given the job. All I had to do was to go in to give my bank details and get my photo taken for my ID. I was very thankful for the new job, but I was also a little worried because I had a speaking engagement for the following week at a Women's Aglow meeting. I told the director about this after I was given the job but she said, "Sure, you can go. Don't cancel it." It was such a blessing to be able to go and minister. God came in such power in the meeting that it surprised me how much He used me in my brokenness! What a merciful Father we have!

Before I spoke, I had been saying to the Lord, "What can I say to people now that my heart has been so broken?" The Lord said, "The invitation came before your husband left. Are you going to go as you were commanded?" I said, "Yes Lord I will go." And so I went. The Lord blessed many women during the meeting, but two women's stories stand out in my mind. Both of them had lost their husbands and were suffering under the weight of their grief. The Lord released them that day and set them free to do as He had commanded. One was set free to go and be a missionary in Ireland. The other woman, a single mother of nine children, met a man the next day who would soon after become her husband. He took care of both her and her nine children, to whom he became a father. How good is our God that He would take the things the enemy meant for harm and turn them into something good?

I still struggled with my own disappointment and sadness over losing my marriage. It was hard not to feel like I had been cheated out of something good. I woke up one Mother's Day feeling sorry for myself, thinking of how other mothers would be spoiled by their husbands for the day. I had to shake myself out of it, so I decided to wash my car, which was parked in front of the house. As I usually did, I started singing to the Lord. As I got carried away, I forgot all about Mother's Day. After a while, a van drove into my driveway and stopped. A man came out with the most beautiful bouquet of flowers I have ever seen. As he was walking towards me, I said, "You have the wrong house." He said, " Are you Deborah Williams?" I said, "Yes, but you have the wrong house." He said, "No, madam, these flowers are for you; I am just a deliverer. The sender's name is on the card. Enjoy your flowers." I took them into the house and looked at the card, which said, "Happy Mother's Day, Deborah. Love from the Lord." WOW! I never did find out who the Lord used to buy me those amazing and beautiful flowers, but I am so thankful to the Lord for making me feel so special and loved. He is so worthy of all praise.

I'm going to stop and pray for you who have just read this part of my story. May the Prince of peace Himself give you peace at all times, in every situation in which you find yourself (2 Thessalonians 3:16). God is pleased with you, no matter where you are in your journey. You don't have to be perfect. Just run into the arms of the Father; His arms are wide open. He is the safest place you can be. He will never let you down. People will fail you sometimes, but God will always be there for you. You are safe in His love and His promises. His promises are "Yes and Amen." His eyes are upon the righteous and His ears are open to their cry. He is never too busy to respond to the cries of His people. You were created to be loved by God and to love Him in return. His love never fails.

# CHAPTER 11

# AMAZING MIRACLES

The day after the Women's Aglow meeting, I went to work. My supervisor was a very nice Baptist lady who was open to learning about the things of the Spirit. In my section of the hospital, I had a patient who was a Jewish woman. She had bowel cancer operation and had to have an attachment of a colostomy bag. She was also blind, so this made it very difficult for her to manage. This was hard for her especially, as she had been a very independent person before she went blind. One morning, she had an accident with her bag, but instead of ringing for help, she tried to clean it herself, which made more of a mess. When she realized she was making things worse, she decided to ring her buzzer for help. When I got there and saw the mess, I was annoyed at first. But after seeing that she had tried to clean it so that I didn't have to, the compassion of the Lord touched my heart. Before cleaning the mess, I cleaned her up first and said to her, "You are a Jew, a daughter of Abraham. You are ripe to receive healing. Will you let me pray for you?" She said, "Yes, please." I prayed for her and asked if she would like to receive her Messiah. She said, "Yes." I led her to the Lord, and left her room. I continued with my work. The next day I went to see her and asked, "How have you been since I prayed for you yesterday?" She said to me with joy in her voice, "I went to the toilet normally this morning. I am going to go and tell my doctor to close the hole." I was over the moon with joy. We hugged and rejoiced together. I went and told my supervisor about what the Lord had done. Her eyes grew wide and we too hugged and praised the Lord.

Six months later, I wanted to go to a charismatic conference in Adelaide, which was an 18-hour drive from Sydney. I did not have the means to go, but I believed the Lord for provision to go. I kept the registration form until 11:00 PM the night before the conference started. At 11:30 PM my phone rang. It was a young lady who had been blessed in one of my meetings. She said to me, "You don't know me by name, but I was very blessed in your meeting a month ago. I have just heard that you want to go to Adelaide. My husband and I are driving to Adelaide tomorrow at 7:00 AM. If you can be ready by then, we can pick you up and take you with us. The only thing is that we can't bring you back; we are going to have holidays with my sister who lives down there. But you can stay with us at my sister's house during the conference. My husband and I are not attending the conference, but I can drive you to and from the conference. We'll take care of your breakfasts and lunches, too. I don't want any money from you. All I want is that you pray with me every morning before you go to the conference." I was so excited and said, "Yes please. If the Lord can take me there, He can bring me back. I will pack my suitcase now and I will be ready for you to pick me up at 7:00 AM." She said, "You're on." At 7:00 AM the next morning, they were at my door. I left with them not knowing how I was going to come back, but I trusted Daddy to bring me home since He had opened the door for me to go.

My young friend's sister's house was by the beach. It was summer, so it was not hard to get up early to go pray with her at the beach. We really enjoyed this time we had to pray together. One morning, on our way back from the beach, the Lord said, "I want you to fly back to Sydney." I told my friend what I had just heard. She just smiled and said, "Knowing you, you will fly." I felt encouraged that she believed me. When we got to the house, I told her husband about the Lord's plan to fly me home. He was not a believer, so he said, "I will call the train station and see if I can book you on the train because we're leaving tomorrow." I said, "No, the Lord wants me to fly." He knew that I didn't have money even for the train. He tried to call the train station, but no one picked up the phone. He said, "I can't understand it. It's such a big station, why will no one pick up the phone?" I said, "It's because the Lord wants me to fly." He said to me, "Deborah, if you fly, I will become a believer." I said, "Then shake hands on it, because you are going to become a believer. I am flying back to Sydney."

During the first sessions of the conference, we listened to Floyd McClung from YWAM teach on hearing the voice of God. During his talk, he told each of us to find a partner, someone we didn't know, and get a word from the Lord for each other. When I turned to look for someone, my eyes connected with this lady from the far corner of the room. We had a perfect word for each other. After speaking with her a little more, I learned that she was the wife of one of the pastors who was serving as a master of ceremonies. She asked me if I was with someone at the conference and I told her that I was by myself. Then she said to me, "Well, you are no longer going to be by yourself. Come and sit with me. From now on you will have a seat with me." So from that morning on, I had a reserved seat. I didn't need to have a packed lunch anymore because I got to have my meals with the conference speakers. The funny thing is that one of the speakers was a powerfully anointed man from South Africa. Because I was always with the conference speakers, people automatically assumed that I was his wife. Several people would come to me and say, "I was so blessed by your husband's ministry." At first I corrected them, saying that he was not my husband. But so many people kept approaching me that, rather than explaining over and over again, I just said, "Thank you." The pastors and I had a good laugh over it!

At the end of the service, one of the worship leaders and his wife came and asked me to stay at their house until I went home to Sydney. They knew that I was relying on the Lord to fly me back there and they wanted to be part of the miracle when it happened. At lunchtime the next day, I said to his wife, "Tomorrow morning, we are going to pick up my ticket so I'd better ask your husband to book me a ticket." She said to me, "I thought you didn't have the money to fly." I said, "I don't, but Daddy does and He will provide." She and her husband laughed, but I said again, "Please call and book my ticket. Tomorrow, you will not be laughing but celebrating with me." The husband said, "If you get it, I will come home for lunch and celebrate with you." I said, "Then you will see my ticket at lunchtime tomorrow." He did call and was told that there was only one seat left, so he booked it for me.

The next day I got up early, showered, and ate breakfast. I said to my friend, "Get ready. We are going to town to pick up my plane ticket." She said, "Wow, okay." Then there was a knock on the door. She answered it and then called out, "Deborah, you have a visitor, come to the door." I asked her to bring them in, but she insisted that I come to the door. When I got there, there was a gentleman standing on the doorstep in a business suit. He took out a little envelope from his jacket pocket and said, "Deborah, this is for your ticket from the Lord." I said, "Thank you, thank you! I don't know what to say!" He said, "You do not need to say anything; it's written all over your face." I ran back into the bedroom, knelt down and thanked the Lord. My friend called her husband to let him know that the money for the ticket had come and that we were on our way to the city to pick up the ticket. He came home for lunch and we all celebrated together. That testimony released them to step out into the business that they had felt the Lord had called them to, but they had been too afraid to start. I am glad to also let you know that Philip became a Christian. You never know what your one step of faith can do. Your testimony can release faith into others.

# CHAPTER 12

# TIME TO LAY IT ALL DOWN

When I came back from Adelaide, there was a letter from my husband reiterating that he wanted to sell our houses and everything in them. I went back to work and tried to focus instead on my daughter's upcoming wedding. The wife of one of my male patients knew that my daughter was engaged to be married, so one day, she gave me $500 in cash. She said, "I don't want you to pay bills with this money; I want you to buy something nice to wear at your daughter's wedding. I want you to look your best." So I went to a boutique in town and found that they were having a sale at 70 percent off. I found a beautiful dress and shoes with a hat to match. I looked so stunning that one didn't have to ask which lady was the mother of the bride! The Lord took care of everything: a professional cake designer from our church offered to make the wedding cake and the church offered to take care of the wedding reception feast. It did not cost me a penny. We feasted on food and drinks of all kinds and had a great deal of leftovers. The Lord is so good to us!

After the wedding, I had to turn my attention back to the situation with my husband. I was advised to go and see a lawyer to see if I could get my share of the money that Bob had already taken out of the bank and also from the proceeds from the upcoming sales of our homes. I made an appointment to see the lawyer. He was an honorable and well-respected Christian man. He said to me, "Because your husband closed the account, we have no way of getting the money back without taking him to court." I said to him, "I will pray about this and then I will get back to you." I went to the Lord and said, "I need to know what to do here. Do I take my husband to court?" As I was praying, I was going through my Bible and came to Matthew 5: 38-42, "I tell you not to resist an evil person. Turn another cheek, give your second tunic, and go another mile. If he wants your tunic, give it to him." I said, "Lord, this is my life we are talking about here. I have worked hard for what I have. I really need to know what to do. Do I go to court or not? Please make it as clear as day for me. I need to hear from You, Lord." By then it was the eleventh hour. I needed to give my answer the next day as to whether I was going to go to court or not. After midnight, I read (Proverbs 25:8), which says "Do not go to court." I said, "Alright, Lord, I am going to trust You to take care of me. I will let go of everything. I choose to drink the cup of suffering. Even though I don't understand, I choose to love You Lord. Not what I want, but what You want. I don't accuse You for what is happening. I trust you to have a solution to what is going on. So I reject disappointment and I hold on to You. I know what You promised is what You will do. I believe it with all my heart. The one thing I ask of You Lord, the thing I seek most is that I may live in Your house all the days of my life, delighting in Your beauty, Lord, and meditating in Your Temple.' When You said, 'Seek My face,' my heart said to You, 'Your face, Lord, I will seek.' You have been my help. Do not leave me nor forsake me now, O God of my salvation (Psalm 27:4, 8-9). Lord, I position myself to catch a greater measure of the wind of your Spirit. Draw me to where there is no return. I want Your Presence more than anything else. I want to know Your goodness and to see Your glory. I want Your beauty to be seen upon me. I want to diffuse Your fragrance wherever I go. I want to see Your Kingdom come. Oh that all men may know that You, whose name alone is the Lord, are the Most High God over all the earth. I will trust in Your power to deliver me. I will trust in Your wisdom to perfect me, for You know what is best for me. I will trust in Your goodness and mercy. You are the great defender of my heart. The power of Your love is beyond my understanding. The power of Your blood defeats the enemy. Your Spirit lives within me and helps me to think Your thoughts. So I let Him be my positive focus. As my thinking goes, so goes my entire being."

The Lord was calling me to a life of constant communion with Him. The basic training included learning to live above my circumstances. He was teaching me to talk to Him about every aspect of my day, including my feelings. He told me that my ultimate goal was not to control or fix everything around me; it was to keep communing with Him, asking His Spirit to guide me moment by moment. He would keep me close to Him and make my path straight.

The Lord gave me peace about my decision not to go to court as an assurance that He was going to be with me. I went and told my lawyer that I was going to let go of everything and let my husband take whatever he wanted. He asked me if I was sure, and I told him that I was. I prayed only that the Lord would not allow the family home to be sold until my youngest daughter was married. She was engaged at the time, and they already had set a date for their wedding. She had wanted to get ready with her bridesmaids and take pictures in her own home, and I wanted this for her. But as the bridal party car left, I saw the estate agent's car coming to put a "For Sale" sign on the property. I stopped and told them that I refused to let them put it there on my daughter's wedding day and asked that they come another day. They apologized and left.

The Lord was gracious to us during this difficult process. I prayed that He would send a buyer to the house rather than us having a stream of people coming in and out to look at it. He granted my petition by sending a young couple that came to see the house and ended up buying it. My husband came and took everything that he wanted out of the house, including some beautiful antique furniture that I had especially loved.

While I was waiting for the sale of the house to close, I went to our other house for the weekend. It was on the coast about three hours outside of Sydney. I arrived at 10:00 at night and found that my husband had changed the lock on the front door. I didn't know what to do, as it was a weekend and it was dark, with the only light coming from the moon. The children next door were still out riding their bikes with their friends. When my neighbor's son saw me struggling to open the door, he said, "I saw your husband changing the lock. But I think we can help you. My friend's father is a locksmith." They left me and went to his friend's house. They came back with a bunch of keys and tried to open the door but none of the keys fitted. They decided to sit down and think of what else they could do to help me get into the house. When we sat on the window ledge, one of the boys leaned back and cracked one of the windows. Then one of them said, "There you are, you can get in." Wow! God sent His angels. Once I was able to get in, I pushed the dresser against the broken window and went to sleep.

Early the next morning, I had my quiet time with the Lord, thinking about how much this house meant to me. It had been a gift to me from the Lord. We first went to the South Coast on holidays with friends from church. We went there for three years before we could afford to buy our own holiday house. We liked the area, so we kept going there during the summer months. We eventually decided that it would be a good investment to buy our own place there. So when we were next on holiday, I went looking for the estate agents to see how much land was going for. I saw that there was some land for sale in the area we liked. The owner was asking for $32,000 and had refused to take $20,000. So when I offered $11,000, all the estate agents laughed at me except one. After this meeting, I went to the land, stood on it, and prayed: "Lord, I would like to own this land. Dad, can I have it? Can it be mine?" I felt peace come on me, almost like the Lord was saying, "It's yours."

The next morning as I was praying, I had a vision of a couple leaning into the trunk of their car putting their shopping in. I walked over to them, led them to the Lord, and then the vision finished. I had planned to call the real estate agent who did not laugh at my offer, but instead felt that I ought to go meet with him in person. I had a friend staying with me at the time, I told her about the vision and that I was planning to go into town. She said, "Well, I am not going to miss out on the fun by staying here. I will come with you." My friend needed to go to the bank, so I went to the supermarket. While I was there, a lady came out with a little girl sitting in a cart and a toddler walking beside her. The little girl called out, "Mummy, Mummy, look at a black lady!" Her mother was so embarrassed that she didn't know where to look. So I walked up to her and said to her, "You don't need to be embarrassed. How many times do you see a black lady in this town? It's okay, I am not offended." Then I said to the little girl, "What's your name?" She said, "Rebecca." I said to her brother, "And what's your name?" He said, "David." I said, "Oh, biblical names, are you Christians?" The mother said, "Yes, we are. We sponsor a child in Africa." I said, "Wow, that is wonderful that you do that. But do you mind if I explain to you what it means to be a Christian?" She said, "No, I don't mind at all." So I did and asked her if she would like to receive Jesus as her Lord and Savior and become a Christian. She said, "Yes." So I led her in the prayer of repentance and she received the Lord, right there in the supermarket.

My friend met me at the door not long after. When I told her about what happened, she said, "I am not going to let you out of my sight. I don't want to miss out again." I said to her, "Okay, let's go talk to the real estate agents. I have found the lady [from my vision], now I am looking for the man." So we walked into the real estate office and went straight up to the desk of Max, the man who had not laughed at me. He said, "Hello, Deborah, please sit down." I said, "Max, before we talk about earthly business, I am first here to talk about kingdom business. God loves you so much. Do you know that?" He said, "Ah, I hope so." I said, "God sent me here today so you can know so." He asked me, "What shall I do?" I said, "I can lead you in a prayer of repentance and you can receive Jesus as your Lord and Savior. Would you like that?" He said, "Yes, please. After this, how can I refuse?" Right there and then he received the Lord.

Then I said, "Now that we have finished with heavenly business, we can talk about earthly business. Max, can you call the owner of lot 18 and make an offer for me, please? I have been to the land and I know that that land is mine." Max reminded me that the owner was set on selling at the full price of $32,000; he had already refused a $20,000 offer. I repeated, "Max, I know that the land is mine. Please call him." I asked him to put in my offer of $11,000 to the owner and told Max that I would call him the following day. Max did not seem very convinced, but he promised that he would make the call. When we got back to the house, I contacted the pastor of the church that we attended down there whenever we were in town and told him about the two people who had just given their lives to the Lord. He told me that these two people were very influential in the world of sports in that city and that they had been trying to reach them for years. I said, "Well, now you have the privilege of looking after them," and gave him their phone numbers.

Then the next day about lunchtime, I called Max to hear about my offer. He said, "Wow, you won't believe this." I said, "I believe it. Max, I believe! Tell me, he took my offer, didn't he?" He said, "Yes, he will take $13,000." I called my husband and we agreed to buy it. On that property, we built a beautiful home where we enjoyed many holidays with friends and family. We were able to bless other families by allowing them to stay there during the school holidays and weekends if they could not afford a holiday away from Sydney. I was able to spend several weekends there, connecting with the Lord. It truly was His gift to me.

While I was thinking through all of this, I felt the Lord saying, "Pick up all your things and be out of the house by 11:00 AM. You shall not return to this house." I picked up everything I had and put it in my car. I cleaned the house to make it ready for Bob to sell.

I was glad I had listened to the Lord because on my way home I saw his car driving down there. I don't know what would have happened to me if he had found me there. I didn't have the court order with me to stop him from coming near me, because I was not expecting him to see him there. When the time came to let go of the house, I had to pray and ask Daddy to help me surrender the gift that He had miraculously given me. It was easier to surrender the house in Sydney, which was worth a lot more money. It was not so much the value of the house but what it had meant to me. As difficult as it was to let it go, I grew immensely through that experience.

After the settlement of the house in Sydney went through, I had to move. I didn't want to move in with my daughter, as she and her husband had just gotten married. They were able to keep a few boxes of my belongings; I didn't own much by then. My church owned a retirement village, so after a couple of weeks, they let me move into one of the empty apartments. They only charged me a small amount of rent, which was a blessing to help me get back on my feet again.

One Sunday morning, while I was sitting in church, I realized that I had only five dollars to my name, hardly any petrol in the car, and no idea how I was going to get to work that week. When the offering bag was passed around, I took out my purse and said, "Lord, You know that this is all I have and I give it to You." So when the bag came to me, I put the five dollars in. At the end of the service, the senior pastor's wife, who was a prophetess, called me out and told me to stand up in the front next to her. Then she said to the congregation, "I feel the Lord is saying, 'Everyone with money in your pocket, come and give it to her.'" That morning, I left the church with $1,668. How awesome is our God!

# CHAPTER 13

# SURPRISED BY THE HOLY SPIRIT

In 1987, during a time of renewal in pockets of the Body of Christ, the leader of the Vineyard Movement, John Wimber, and his team came to give a conference. I remember the first time that I went to one; I was in Bible school at the time and hungry for more of God. God used to give John the meaning of the different manifestations of the Holy Spirit before they even started happening. He would say, "The Holy Spirit is coming into that section," and explain what was going to be happening to the people that God was going to touch. One afternoon, he pointed to the section where I was standing and said, "The Spirit is coming into that section. You all are going to find your body shaking from the waist up; this is the Holy Spirit creating a hunger for the Word of God." As the Spirit descended, my top half shook like a reed while my lower part stood stiff as a board. I believe that I did receive a new hunger for the Word that day; it was amazing. God continued to move in that conference and during all the conferences they gave in Australia. People were being baptized in the Holy Spirit, healed of afflictions, and delivered from demons. It was beautiful to be there and witness all this. God used John to demolish denominational barriers in our nation. Many pastors returned to their churches hungry for the things of the Spirit in their own churches. Some even lost their jobs because their congregations were not open to the Spirit. Most of them chose to continue seeking the Lord and started their own ministries. John Wimber believed in equipping the saints to do the work of the ministry; he called it "doing the stuff." He also taught power evangelism, or prophetic evangelism as we called it then. We would learn about all this and then be released to go and evangelize in the market places. I will be forever grateful for how much I learned from that man's ministry. John taught about the Father's heart. He is a man who left a legacy for his generation, which is still blessing people everywhere.

A few years later my friend and I went to the Voice of Victory Convention in Melbourne. Kenneth Copeland was the speaker that night. After the worship, he said, "Open your Bibles to Psalm 112." When he said that, the uncontrollable joy of the Lord hit me in my belly like a ton of bricks; I was paralyzed drunk. Kenneth tried to read "Psalm 112" multiple times. Every time he did, it was as if God blew His breath on me, making me drunker and drunker in the Spirit until I could not sit up. But the funny thing is that when my friends touched me, trying to help me back on the chair they got drunk too. Even those who could reach me with just one tip of their finger became drunk. I was saturated with the Holy Spirit; my cup was overflowing. The whole center section was under the power of the Holy Spirit. Within minutes, the whole stadium started filling up with laughter. Kenneth called out saying, "I feel like God is saying, 'Kenneth, give up, and let Me do what I want to do." Then he said, "You, sister, who started all this, God is saying that you are to get to the lady at the end of your row and lay hands on her. Even if you have to crawl to get there, even if they have to carry you, you must lay your hands on her." I could only go on my hands and knees. As I crawled, people were pushing me along and also becoming drunk after they touched me. When I finally got to the lady, I saw that she was very pregnant. I think she had been given bad news about the baby because she was crying. But I was so drunk in the Spirit that I couldn't stop laughing. I plunked my head on her big tummy and laughed and laughed until she broke into laughter as well. When what needed to be done was done, the Spirit threw me off of her and across the room, as if someone had literally picked me up and threw me. What's amazing is that I did not experience any pain. I got up laughing and crying at the same.

By that time, joy had spread until it filled the entire stadium. People were being healed left, right, and center. Some were getting out of their wheelchairs. One lady lost twenty pounds. So many people there were saved. I have never before (or after) seen a stadium so full of people drunk in the Holy Spirit. Many of us left the stadium still very drunk. When we stepped into the tram, the joy spread to everyone inside. My friends and I had to be helped by unbelievers out of the tram into our hotel. When we got in the elevator, we were still laughing. One lady said to me, "Have you been to see the show Cats?" I said, "No, lady, we have been to see the Big Cat!" She said, "Oh, what is that?" I said, "The Big Cat is the Lion of the tribe of Judah. And tomorrow it's on again if you would like to come; it's free admission."

I had already been part of the ministry team in my church. But I didn't realize that I had received a powerful anointing from the Lord during the convention. The following Sunday during the ministry time in my church, the people I approached were falling under the power of the Holy Spirit before I could pray for them. The senior pastor had been standing on the platform at the front of the church, watching what was happening. He could not believe what he was seeing. He sent another pastor to follow me to see if I was pushing people down, but they could see that I wasn't. I was not new to the church. These people knew me, which is why they were asking me to pray for them to receive healing.

When the power of God came upon me, I would tremble and the palms of my hands would shake. I would try to sit on my hands to stop them from shaking, but when I did, my head would spin and joy would fill me up. Some people would ask me, "Where is that in the Bible?" I knew they loved me, and I didn't want to be deceived either, so I would ask, "Lord, where is this in the Bible?" The Lord was gracious showed me things in the Bible. For example, in Daniel 10:10-11, Daniel had an encounter with God that left him trembling. So I would share with them what the Lord had given to me.

I was still hungry for more of God, so I began attending meetings at another church where Rodney Howard-Browne, a pastor from the U.S., had been ministering. I got so drunk in the first meeting that I went to, that I began to laugh uncontrollably and had to be driven home. The meetings went on for a couple of weeks, after which we had a conference in our own church. My pastor came to me, excited to tell me that he had heard that there was a lady from Zimbabwe coming with her husband to our conference. She'd heard of me as well, so we were both looking forward to meeting one another. What's funny is that I was expecting that she'd be a black lady and she was expecting that I'd be a white lady. It was a most awkward moment for both of us. I thought that I had dealt with the pain of the white people's racism before I left Rhodesia, as it was known then. But to my surprise, it was still there. Despite the fact that I had married a white man, I didn't know that I still struggled with this issue. So I said to the Lord, "I don't want this in my life, Lord. Help me to totally forgive and be healed." I found out later that she was experiencing the same thing. I looked for her the next day, but could not find her. I thought instead that I would just pray through it with the Lord and that it would be done with.

A few months later, I went to another John Wimber conference where I attended an Evangelism workshop. When I got to the room where it was to be held, I found out that the pastor leading it was a white South African man. Now I had a choice: confront this thing and deal with it once and for all, or allow it to continue to rob me. I decided that I was going to deal with it. So I waited until after the class finished and then told him what was going on with me and that I wanted to pray for reconciliation. He agreed, saying that he had had issues about it himself. So together we did reconciliation and put that pain to death. For the rest of the conference, we were brother and sister. When I got back home, I contacted the white Zimbabwean lady and did the same thing with her. Later on in the year, our church had a ladies' retreat where I shared my testimony. The Lord used it to bring reconciliation between Australians and the Aboriginal people. I didn't know it at the time, but the Lord was preparing me to be involved in the reconciliation of people groups and nations, which I will write more about it in the following chapters.

# CHAPTER 14

# THE TURNING OF A NEW PAGE

When I discovered there was a new release of land for sale, I felt it was time to start turning a new page, begin a new life, and buy land. Many people from our church had bought land already in this area. The trouble was that you could not just go and buy it. Because the land was so popular, it was being sold by ballot. If your number came out, then you could choose the plot you wanted. You did have the option of listing your preferences before the ballots were due. The night before the ballots were drawn, I had a dream about the number 18, which was not the number on my preference papers. The next day, my friend went with me to the ballot draw. While the man was climbing up the ladder to write the numbers on the board, I turned to my friend and said softly to her, "The number I was given in the dream is different to what's on my preference papers they have. I wonder if they will let me change it." Before my friend could answer me, the man up the ladder shouted, "Don't worry if the number on your preference papers is different. It all just depends on when your number comes out. Then you can choose what plot you want if it's not taken yet." So my friend said, "There is your answer."

The man came down and turned the barrel. Out came my number first. So I was able to buy the plot in my dream, number 18.

Once we bought the land, we had to build on it within twelve months or sell it back to the developer. Getting the bank to lend me the money to build the house was going to be a challenge. My daughter Hazel had been working for a while, I asked her to help me by putting both our names on the loan, though I would be paying it off. The bank said, "Once the house is finished and we put a value on it, you can take her name off the loan." I was happy about that; I didn't want my loan to be a burden on her when she and her husband got married and bought their own home. Twelve months came and went, but I had not yet begun to build on the land. I got a phone call from an Anglican minister saying, "You got choice land. That was the plot of land we wanted." They bought their second preference. I knew then that the Lord had gone before me by giving me the dream, but I also knew that I would have to contend to keep it. So after twelve months I went to the property manager's office to see if they could give me an extension. The man said, "Deborah, you got choice land. If you lose it, you will never be able to get it back; the land prices are shooting up every two months. My advice would be to write a letter to the manager and ask for an extension." I followed his advice and was given an extension. Another year came and went, but I still did not start construction for the house. People started dumping rubbish on my land as they built around me, even leftover concrete from building their swimming pools. The manager said, "Deborah, it is your responsibility to clean your land if you want to have an extension and keep your land. People would not be dumping on it if you had built your house." I agreed, and my friend's husband went and cleaned it up for me.

The Lord is never too late. The final warning to build came on a Friday afternoon and by the following Monday, I had received the approval for my loan from the bank. So I was able to call the property manager's office and tell them that I could now build my home. The manager was so happy for me that he offered to drive me in his new car to show me how to position my house in order to get the best benefit of the sun.

## *My dream house*

I went to a building company that I had seen the first time after I bought the land. The lady there was so nice and happy to see me. She said to me, "Do you realize it's been two years now? But I really want to look after you. I still have your papers. The prices have gone up since we talked last, but I will talk to my boss and see if he can still give you the price I first gave you." I asked if they would still give me the special items that were included with the house. She said, "Yes, I will ask my boss not to change anything." The boss agreed, so I signed the contract and went to pick up my bricks. That night, I had a dream that I was standing outside of my completed house, admiring how nice it looked. I noticed then that it was built with different bricks than the ones that I had just chosen. These were sandstock bricks, which are nicer, more expensive bricks. The house looked simply beautiful. The next morning, I called the brick company and asked if I could change the bricks. They agreed to give them to me at no extra cost. Then I asked what the name was of those bricks and was told that it was called Endeavor. I looked up the meaning of endeavor and found out that it means "to try hard to do or achieve something, do one's best, do one's utmost, give one's all, going beyond what is required." Wow, how wonderful is our Daddy! He is interested in every minute detail of our lives, even down to the bricks I would use to build my house with. He wanted a beautiful home for His princess. He only gives the best.

After the house was built, I put down a deposit to have the driveway done. The following Sunday while I was in church, the pastor asked, "Who would like to go to Toronto and Brownsville revival?" I was the only one who raised my hand to go. Then he said, "Okay, we'll need $300 by Wednesday to hold our spots." The next day when I went to work, the supervisor said that they were going to have to cut down on staff. When I left the office I said, "Listen here, devil, you are going to watch me walk on my driveway AND you are going to watch me get on that plane." The next morning, I got a call from my friend Deborah who asked, "Are you home right now, and if yes, can I drop in and give you something?" I said, "Yes, I am home." She came and said, "I don't know what this is about, but the Lord told me to give you this." She gave me an envelope with the $300 I needed for the deposit for my trip. I knew then that God wanted me to go. Finances were His business. He was going to take care of all of it, including spending money. He was going to complete what He had started (Philippians 1:6). I am glad to tell you that every penny came for Brownsville, for Toronto, and even for Disneyland; I even had money to eat in the restaurant in the Revolving Dining Room in Niagara Falls, Ontario. God even delivered me from the fear of heights while I was in Disneyland so I wouldn't miss out on the fun.

### When the King of Glory Came in the Room

We had people from other churches join our team on this trip, so there ended up being 31 of us. The night before we left, they prayed for us all together. I was nervous because I had not been very fond of flying. While we were praying, I went down under the power of the Holy Spirit. I said to the Lord, "Please take away this horrible, ill feeling I have about flying." The Lord said, "Deborah, you might as well get used to flying, because you are going to be doing a lot of it." I am so glad to say that He took away that horrible feeling I had about flying. By now, I have been able to take the gospel of Jesus Christ to 31 countries and have loved it.

Revival had broken out in our church in Sydney Australia at the same time as it did in Catch The Fire church in Toronto Canada, known world wide as the Toronto Blessing. Many people were coming to drink of the living water. I volunteered to clean the toilets. I loved doing it, especially the men's toilets, because nobody liked cleaning the men's toilets. While I cleaned, I used to pray that there would be no safe place to hide from the presence of God. We heard testimonies of people being zapped by the Spirit of the Lord when they thought they would go and hide in the toilets. People were being healed in worship without anyone praying for them. I was permanently drunk for three and a half years, even as I traveled to different countries. The team had to help carry my bags and me. Thank You, Lord that we were treated as VIPs in Brownsville and in Toronto. We didn't have to line up with the masses.

We had experienced a measure of the glory of God one night in worship at our church back in Australia. When the glory filled the house, there was a sudden hush. You could have heard a pin drop. All of us were pulling up our long pants because it felt like there was water rising. Nobody spoke. The second time I experienced the glory was during a conference in another church in Sydney, which was also a drinking hall. They had invited an older lady from the USA whom we could tell knew the Lord. After worship, while we were all still standing, she was invited to the stage where she was introduced and handed the microphone. As the words, "He is here" left her mouth, everyone fell flat on their faces. He had come all right. Everyone in the room could feel it. No one was standing. Again there was such a hush that nobody moved or spoke. There was dead silence for what seemed like an eternity. But every one of us was busy searching our own hearts. You just felt that you had to check your own heart to make sure there was nothing out of line with the Lord. You could not afford to allow anything that was not right to remain. It was intense. It was even more intense than the two times the Lord set our church building on fire. A helicopter was flying overhead, saw the fire and called the fire brigade. When the fire brigade came, they searched but could not find a trace of the fire. It was a phenomenon. Many people today do not believe that it is possible to encounter the living God like it was in the old days. But it is possible and He is just waiting for us to call on Him to show up. And show up He will!

There were many, many people who had come to Brownsville to drink the living water, so there would be people waiting in
line from 8:00 AM for a service at 7:00 PM. But we were treated
like VIPs and didn't have to wait in line; we were able to come right
inside. The revival there was amazing. It created unbelievable hunger
for God in the hearts of many people both near and far, believers
and unbelievers alike. People were actually flying in from all over the
world to be saved. When you stepped into the sanctuary, you could
feel the weightiness of His glory and the awesome fear of His holi-
ness. You knew you had entered into the presence of a Holy God.
Everyone I know who went there went up to the altar on their first
day; we were compelled to confess every sin just to make sure we
didn't miss anything. When it was time for the salvation call, people
ran for their lives to the altar to be saved. Everyone ran and bowed
their knees. It was a perfect image of what the Bible describes: "Every knee will bow and every tongue confess that Jesus Christ is Lord,
to the glory of the Father."

In Toronto, the emphasis was on the "Father" Heart of God.
It was and still is about people coming into a deep revelation of the
Father's love as His sons and daughters. It was and still is about the
healing of the church, allowing her to come into her identity and
into an intimate relationship with the Bridegroom. They spoke of
soaking in the presence of God or allowing His fire to burn what
could be burned out of our lives. I wanted all God had for me. I let
Him do what He needed to do in me: burning what needed to be
burned out and filling me to overflowing with His fire of love. I want
to be a burning, shining light, a flame that lights many fires. Whatever fire touches, it changes. Many lives were transformed. There
were marriages that were on the verge of divorce but were healed as
the couples got drunk together on the carpet. I loved every minute
that I was there. We were there for ten days. We spent time with the
leaders of different departments seeing how they operated. It was
very inspiring to learn new ways of doing things as the Spirit led.

In both Toronto and home, we found that the secret to

maintaining revival was cultivating a hunger for more of God's presence and glory; soaking, worshiping, and interceding brought us into greater intimacy with the Lord. The presence of the Lord became tangible. When we were in Toronto, I chose to attend a workshop on prayer and fasting, which was led by Lou Engle. He was already on fire and had done 40-day fasts more than once. He taught us how to be passionate about intimacy with the Lord and intercession. The following year, we invited him and Stacey Campbell to do a youth conference at our church in Australia. The worship was charged with the presence of God. All of a sudden, I went into an encounter with the Lord. I was sitting on a huge dining table fit for a king. It was full of exotic, delicious food and drinks of all kinds. As I was eating this amazing food, the Lord said, "Eat as much as you want. This is all for you. You will never starve again." I ate and drank to my heart's content. But the food on the table did not decrease. The table looked like it had not been touched. When I came out of that encounter, I knew that I had been healed of the childhood pain of being starved by my stepmother. I had not been thinking about the years of my youth. But it's amazing when you abandon yourself in worship. The Lord knows the right time to heal different areas of our live. I can't explain it, but I knew that I had been healed in that area of my life in a youth conference. There, the Lord gave me a promise that I would never starve again.

The next day again in worship, I went into another encounter with the Lord. This time, I was about seven or eight years old. I was dressed in a beautiful, colorful dress. The skirt was full, like the flair of the 1960s. Jesus led me by the hand to the huge throne where Daddy was sitting. Jesus was showing me off to Daddy saying, "Isn't she beautiful? Isn't she gorgeous? Daddy, isn't she beautiful?" I was holding my pretty dress out, showing it off. Daddy was smiling and nodding His head, saying, "Yes, she is so beautiful. She is gorgeous." He looked so happy and so proud of me. Then Jesus pulled my hand gently directing me to the door. We ran out together into a field covered with exquisite flowers. As He frolicked with me through the field, I noticed that the flowers were not being trampled. When I came out of that encounter, I knew the Lord had restored my childhood that was robbed from me.

During that conference, Stacey prophesied over me and said, "The Lord wants me to lay hands on you to stir up a gift in you. He has called you to be a prophet like me. He has called you to preach and prophesy, to dream dreams and to interpret. Now go, preach and prophesy."

It was also during that conference that Lou Engle announced the first prayer gathering called THE CALL, in Washington DC, which some of our youth attended. We saw God doing amazing things. One man had a heart implant right on the platform while we all watched; we could literally see something like hands moving under his shirt. He was acting as though he was under a general anesthetic. The next day he went to the doctor for a checkup. The doctor told him that he had a new heart like that of a 20-year-old.

One morning during a meeting in our church in Australia, weeks after the conference, a woman came and asked me to pray with her for her husband who was now in the nursing home suffering from dementia. She chose to put him there after the dementia had caused such confusion in him that she could not take care of him anymore. After I prayed she said, "I feel that I ought to go to the nursing home and bring him tonight." She left to go get him and bring him back to the conference. While we were worshiping, she looked at her lifted up hands and saw that her fingers were perfectly straight. She had had arthritis in her fingers, but the Lord healed her. At the time of the altar call for salvation, her husband got up and walked to the front. His wife said, "When he got up and started walking to the front, I thought to myself, 'I am not going to stop him. I will watch to see what he will do.'" He ended up giving his heart to the Lord that day. After the service, his wife took him home instead of taking him back to the nursing home. He lived another two years at home until he died naturally. Wow! The things I have seen God do are amazing.

A month or so later, we held a conference for pastors in our church in Australia. I prayed for many couples that went down in the Spirit. While one particular couple went down on the floor, the Lord told the wife to take off her ring, which was 18-carat gold ring with nine diamonds, and give it to me. When she got up, she told her husband what she just heard. They had planned to leave after that night's session, but she told her husband that she wanted to stay another night to make sure that what she heard was from the Lord. She told me later that she said, "Lord, this ring is 18-carat gold with nine diamonds!" He said, "Yes, take it off and give it to her." She said, "I thought to myself, 'On Monday, the pastors have their day off. I will come back tomorrow, and if she is here I will know that it was the Lord. If she is not here, I get to keep my ring.'" So she came back, but didn't ask the receptionist if I was there. I was in the prayer chapel when she first came, thanking the Lord for what He had done in the conference. When she didn't find me, she thought, "Good, I get to keep my ring." But as she was going through the front door to the parking lot, I saw her from behind. I ran after her and asked her if everything was all right, wondering why she had come back; I thought that they had left the night before. Then she said, "Oh, you are here! Show me your finger." I did. She took off the ring and put it on my finger and said, "Oh, it doesn't fit." I said, "Oh yes it does," pushing it into position. As I went to take it off, she said, "The Lord told me to give it to you after you prayed for us yesterday. But I wanted to make sure it was the Lord. That's why I am here." I tried to give it back but she said, "Please don't take it off. It's your gift from the Lord." I thanked her and she left.

I did not tell anyone about this beautiful gift. Instead, I started to ask the Lord, "Why a ring with nine diamonds?" But I did not get an answer until Sunday morning. I used to get to church early so I could pray before the service. When I got off the floor and sat down, a man walked in and lay down on the floor praying. After a time, he turned around and said, "Deborah, the Lord is saying, 'The nine diamonds are the nine gifts; I am increasing your gifts.'" This man knew nothing about the ring. Wow, Lord, thank you! I still have the ring today as a reminder to me of His loving-kindness, which is better than life.

## Taking the Fire to the Nations

While I was in Bible school, the Lord started opening doors in different churches, denominations, and countries that were hungry for the fire of revival. My first invitation to speak outside of our church came from an Anglican church in Sydney. When I got there, the Lord started to reveal to me some of the things that were happening among the congregation. After I spoke my message, there was ministry time. After praying for people, the pastor asked me to meet and pray with him and his leadership team. Later, he wrote to me and thanked me for the breakthrough that came in the church as a result of us praying together that day.

My first invitation to speak outside my state of New South Wales was from Mount Beauty in Victoria. It came during a peak time of revival in our church. I invited a friend from my church and my son in-law, George, to go and be the ministry team. We stayed at the pastor's house, which had three bedrooms. This meant that my friend and I had to share a double bed. We didn't mind as we were close friends and both very slim. But to my surprise, when I woke up early in the morning, my friend was sleeping on the floor. I asked her what happened. She said, "I couldn't sleep. I was repenting all night. There was so much fire coming out of you that I had to make sure there was not one sin hidden in my life. I could not be near you in bed." When we went to church, God came in power. He ministered through us in such a powerful way, there was not one person left standing. When we went back to the evening service, the same thing happened. The next day, a couple came to the pastor's house and asked me to pray for the wife's father, who was dying in hospital of cancer. He had been a freemason and a very angry man throughout his life and didn't want to hear about the Lord. We could not go to the hospital with them because we were leaving that morning, so I prayed instead over a prayer cloth and gave it to her to take to the hospital. When she and her husband got to the hospital, she put the prayer cloth on him without saying a word. He said to her, "Tell me about what you have been trying to tell me all this time." She said, "What, Dad?" He said, "You know, uh, about Jesus, you know." Then she said, "Oh, yes, I would love to." Then she led him to the Lord. Not only did the Lord pardon his sin, He healed him from cancer! WOW! He had been very weak and at the point of death. But he gained strength and was sent home completely restored.

After I returned home, I got an invitation to go to Alice Springs in the Northern Territory to do a conference for combined churches. During that conference, there was a woman in attendance who'd been crippled by arthritis. I felt that she had deep seeds of bitterness planted in her. I asked her quietly if she would allow me to ask the Lord to give her grace to forgive the person who had hurt her, to which she agreed. I prayed for her to be physically healed after she forgave the person who had hurt her. We watched the Lord heal those swollen, twisted fingers and restore her feet to normal size. The Lord ministered to many people in that conference, but that woman's healing sticks out most in my memory because I saw again how bitterness could destroy a person's life.

When I came back from Alice Springs, I went to the evening service at my church. That night on my way to the bathroom, a lady said to me, "Would you be our speaker next month?" I said to her, "Can I get back to you on that, please?" She agreed. I thought to myself, "That is a funny way to ask someone to be a guest speaker in your church. This lady doesn't even know if I preach." In the meantime, she was thinking the same thing. After I accepted the invitation, she told me that after asking me to speak, she said to herself, "What have I done? I don't even know if she speaks, and if she does, I don't know if she is the speaker the Lord said He would give to me." She and her husband pastored a church in central coast north of Sydney. They had brought a bus full of their people, mainly young adults, to seek revival and catch the fire in our church. After the service, I told my senior pastor about the invitation. I always asked for their permission before I accepted an invitation to go and preach outside of our church. As I was heading to the parking lot, I ran into our associate pastor and I told him about the invitation as well. He said, "Take it. They are so hungry for the fire of God. That's their bus there, go let them know that you'll be able to accept their invitation." When I went over to the bus, it had started to rain a little. The woman who had asked me to speak came to the door and said, "Come in out of the rain." Then she introduced me to her husband and the members of their congregation as their guest speaker for next month, all before I had even officially accepted the invitation. She told me that the Lord told her to organize a combined meeting for a few different churches and that He would give her the speaker. So after she asked me to be the speaker, she thought to herself, "I hope she is the one the Lord meant. The words came out of my mouth before I even thought of it, and I don't have the venue for the meetings yet!" But the Lord was gracious and provided them with a venue. Just by word of mouth, every meeting was packed out. We went early to prepare for the first session, but by the time we got there, the parking lot was already packed with cars. God was so good. He came in power and many were saved, healed, and baptized in the Holy Spirit. What's incredible is that many came to the meetings who had not been previously open to the Spirit. One man confessed to being a freemason and wanted to be free. He had tried and failed to free himself in the past, but that night he left a free man by the power of the Holy Spirit. Nothing is too hard for our God!

# CHAPTER 15

# OUT-OF-BODY EXPERIENCES

In 1997, I received an invitation to speak in Adelaide, in South Australia. It was after I accepted the invitation that I found out it was another combined churches conference. The first day was going to be for pastors and leaders. I had never led a conference before. I felt like Jeremiah when he said, "Lord you tricked me!" I could not pull out since it had already been organized. The night before I left for Adelaide, while driving to church for the evening service, the Lord said, "Deborah, you don't need to fear. All you have to say when you stand up to speak is, 'I was not disobedient to the heavenly call.'" That was right out of Acts 26:19. I said, "Thank You, Lord." But I was still nervous. That evening, after praying for people who wanted impartation of the fire of revival, I was prayed for and went down in the Spirit. The pastor who prayed for me moved on to pray for other ministry team members. As he passed me still lying on the floor, he said, "Deborah, the Lord is saying, 'When you get to Adelaide you do not need to fear. When you stand to speak to the pastors, all you need to say is, 'I was not disobedient to the heavenly calling.'"

**First out-of-body experience:** When he said that, all of a sudden I had an out-of-body experience. I was suspended in the air over my body. It was like there were two Deborahs. I was looking down at my body. It didn't feel funny or scary; somehow it felt normal. To me, it was a confirmation that He was going with me. He was going to do the impossible and I didn't need to be afraid.

I was obedient to the call and went to the conference. When I was introduced, I honored the pastors who had organized the conference. After I spoke, I said, "How many want the fire of revival?" They all stood and lined up. Then I said, "I was not disobedient to the heavenly calling." Right as I said this, the whole row of pastors fell like dominos under the power of the Holy Spirit. After seeing that, I was confident that God was going to show up in the conference. I am glad to tell you that I was not disappointed.

**The second out-of-body experience:** It was 1998, while I was at a church in Malaysia, during a time of worship. The air was charged with the presence of God. The next thing that happened was that I was taken to another country. It was a Muslim country where I was ministering to a group of women. Most of them were young, but their heads were covered. They were very receptive to the gospel. When I had finished ministering to them and they were free, I was back in my body and continued to worship. As incredible of an experience as that was, it did not seem at all unnatural to me.

**The third out-of-body experience:** While I was in my house alone worshiping. A friend dropped in and joined me in worship. Momentarily, I was taken to another country, but the people were different than the Muslims. They were Asians, but I knew I was not in China because of their dialect. Amazingly enough, I could speak their language too. They welcomed me. After ministering to them, I came back into my body. My friend who had been sitting in the room said, "You went somewhere, didn't you? I could tell that you were not here." So I said, "Yes I did, how did you know?" She said, "You were talking to some people in a language that I didn't understand. I could tell you weren't just praying in tongues; it was a holy moment. I didn't move the whole time that you were having the encounter."

**The forth out-of-body experience:** I was taken to heaven. It happened while we were worshiping in church. All of a sudden, it was as if there was no roof on our church and I realized that I had been taken to heaven. I joined in the worship with people from every tribe and tongue. Every eye was looking up, every tongue was singing, "Holy, Holy, Holy" and every hand was lifted toward the throne in front of us. The worship in heaven was indescribable, and the Godhead was the center of it all. It was so pure and holy. I was trembling like a reed when I came back. My senior pastor saw that I had been somewhere. She held me because I was trembling so much and she put the microphone to my mouth to share with the congregation where I had been. It was not easy to talk about it. I am still awestruck when I remember it.

**The fifth out-of-body experience:** I was again taken to heaven, but this time I was taken to the "spare body parts room." There were body parts hanging down on hooks, like those in an old fashioned butcher shop. As I was wondering why I had been brought to that room, the Lord drew my attention to a heart. I wondered why, as I didn't know anyone with a heart problem. I thought to myself, "Maybe the Lord is going to use me to heal broken hearts." Then the Lord took a heart and placed it into my hands. I asked the Lord, "Who is this for?" but He did not tell me. So I brought the heart with me out of that encounter.

I was a chaplain at two general hospitals in Sydney during that time. I went to one hospital on Tuesdays and the other on Wednesdays. In my quiet time with the Lord on Monday morning the Lord told me to go to the hospital I would normally visit on that morning instead of on Wednesday. I wondered if this had anything to do with the heart, but the Lord did not answer my question that day. Tuesday morning I woke up early, had my quiet time with the Lord as usual, and went to the hospital, still unsure of why He wanted me to stay home the next day. Wednesday morning, the Lord told me to download the FaceTime app (which I had deleted from my iPhone) and call Doug and Donna, two of my friends who live in Canada. When I called, Doug answered on his iPad and told me that Donna had just had a massive heart attack. I could see her all wired up in a small hospital. There had been no warning at all that she had had a heart problem. Right then, everything became clear to me. I told them that the Lord had gone before her during the previous week by taking me to heaven and giving me a heart for her. They asked me to pray that the Lord would open the door for her to be flown to Vancouver, where the best heart specialist was. I said, "Give me two hours. I will pray and get back to you." I hung up and called a prayer partner. I told her why we were going to pray and asked, "Will you agree in prayer about this?" She agreed, and we prayed. When I felt our answer had come, I called Doug and Donna to say that the Lord had made a way for them. Doug said, "Yes, we have just been told that she is scheduled to be flown to Vancouver." Donna was flown to Vancouver Hospital, and was treated by one of their best cardiologists. After the procedure, the cardiologist said, "Donna, you have been given a new heart. What are you going to do with it? People who get this kind of heart attack don't usually survive it." I'm happy to tell you that not only is Donna alive and well, but she is on fire for God. Praise God for His goodness.

The following year they came to visit me in Redding, CA. I told them of a miracle that had happened the previous week in the chair where Doug was sitting. A friend had called me at 10:00 PM crying. She said, "Deborah, I know it's late, but we are desperate. My daughter just got back from the doctor who told her that she is now deaf in one ear and tinnitus in the other. It's driving her crazy, but there is nothing they can do for her. Please, can we come for prayer?" I said, "Yes, come. I am still up." They came and when I prayed for her, her ear popped open and the ringing stopped. Up to this day, she is still healed. Six months later, she sent me an email asking me to pray for her friend who was born deaf. I didn't know when she came to me that she had actually been born without an eardrum. I asked Daddy to send an angel to bring her a new eardrum. He answered my request and healed her. Praise the Lord. After sharing that testimony, Doug said, "I have an ear that doesn't hear either." I said, "The same God who healed Natalie's ear in that chair will heal you too." I commanded his ear to open and pop! It opened!

In 2017, Doug was healed again. He had had a neck problem for about forty years, which the doctors had told him was degeneration and that he would have to live with it; there was nothing they could do about it. I commanded Doug's neck to come into divine alignment and that the neck problem would leave, which it did. Praise You, Lord, that anyone in Your realm can do anything. For with You, nothing is impossible in Jesus' name.

# CHAPTER 16

# SUMMONING NATIONS TO WORSHIP THE KING OF GLORY

The Lord started opening doors outside Australia. I have had the privilege of meeting many high-profile men and women of God through my years of being a minister of the gospel of Jesus Christ. I am a better woman for knowing them. Their input in my life is priceless. Only heaven will tell how grateful I am for what I have learned and gleaned from them. The first country that I was able to minister in was New Zealand, then Malaysia, Singapore, several countries in the Americas, Argentina, Guatemala, Mexico, Israel, Turkey, the U.K., India, Japan, and Colombia. The Lord took me to dangerous islands of the Philippines and the islands of Papua New Guinea (to understand the danger in these islands, continue reading). He also sent me to some of the European countries, and then Israel. There is something special about Israel. As soon as we landed, I felt like I had arrived home. When we came out of the plane and I put my foot on the ground, I felt as if my spirit had leapt within me. I had a sense that I had finally come home. I have been back many times and each time, the feeling is the same.

Then, in 1998, bigger doors started to open. I was already part of the Australian Prayer Network (part of the International Prayer network) when I was invited to be part of the team of prophetic intercessors to represent Australia at the World Congress held in Guatemala. The World Congress was a gathering of Christian leaders, Evangelists and prophetic intercessors to seek the Lord for a breakthrough into nations that were not open to the gospel. It was by invitation only. It was lead by Peter Wagner and Cindy Jacobs. These nations were in what was then called 10/40 Window. The Australian team was lead by Pastor Ben Gray from Brisbane, who was the co-ordinator of the South Pacific region. We had just had Randy Clark as our conference speaker at our church. He was on his way to the Argentinean revival. As he shared about what God was doing there, I had a longing to go there too. So when the invitation came to go to Guatemala, I thought, "This is going to be my opportunity to go to the Argentine revival in South America." I invited a friend to come with me and we booked our tickets to Guatemala, with a scheduled detour through Argentina. God was gracious and gave us favor with an Argentinean couple that attended my friend's church. They had a daughter who was still in Argentina and was serving on Claudio Freidzon's leadership team. They called her and organized it so that we could stay with her. Their daughter Adriana offered to pick us up from the airport and to take us to church, where we were treated as VIPs.

There were many Christian leaders of movements invited to the World Congress, who had the same idea of going to Guatemala through Argentina in order to catch the fire of revival. When we got to the church, it was already packed and there were many people standing in line outside for the next service, worshiping as they waited. When it was our turn to go in, Adriana said, "I forgot that the service is in Spanish; my English is not good enough to translate." As soon as the words left her mouth, she spotted a friend of hers who translated for Cindy Jacobs when she preaches in that church, coming toward us. She said, "Hold on, I will ask her if she can stay and translate for you." When Adriana had asked, her friend pointed to me and said, "Now I know why I am here. It was for you." She lived 1,500 kilometers from where we were in Buenos Aires. The Lord had awoken her husband in the night and told him to buy a ticket and send her to Buenos Aires. When he asked the Lord why she needed to go so urgently, the Lord just repeated what He had told him to do. Her husband was obedient to buy the ticket, and she arrived in the morning. She went to the morning service, but she didn't have peace during that service or the next one. It wasn't until Adriana had asked her to interpret for us that she had peace.

We were ushered to the front seats. The worship was beautiful. They sang in Spanish, but some of the songs we knew in English, so we were able to join in. When the time came to welcome visitors, Claudio welcomed the different leaders of movements in the Body of Christ. We all clapped our hands as they stood up and sat down. Then Claudio said, "I would like the congregation to stand up and welcome my two special friends from Australia." When we stood up, he said, "I don't want you down there, I want you up here with me." By that time, I was already drunk in the Holy Spirit and needed help getting up to the stage. Then he asked me, "I carry an anointing for the nations. Do you want it as well?" I said, "Yes, yes, pleeeeease!" He said, "Take it!" and laid hands on me. As he did, I went down. He said, "Pick her up. Do you want more?" I said, "Yes." He imparted again and again. I felt so full that I thought I was going to burst. But I didn't want to say, "Lord stop." After he prophesied over me, I asked that he would pray for my friend as well. He prayed for her then prayed for me again. We both went flying to the floor and had to be carried off the stage. I was so glad that I didn't have to drive back home that night!

We went back to Adriana's home, along with our interpreter and spent most of that night talking of the goodness of God. We went back on Sunday before leaving for Guatemala and Claudio prayed for me again. We saw him not long after at the World Congress and had the pleasure of seeing him and his wife two months later in Australia.

## The First Prayer Network World Congress, 1998

On our way from Argentina to Guatemala we changed aircrafts in Miami from a jumbo jet to a tiny little plane. My friend was given a seat two rows back from my row, where I sat in the middle seat. I had two gentlemen sitting on either side; one was an unbeliever and the other a Spanish pastor who had also been invited to the World Congress. It was the same year that the hurricane devastated Honduras and part of Guatemala. We had just had our dinner and were approaching Honduras when the plane started going up and down, up and down. I looked at the unbeliever by the window. His eyes were shut tight and his face pressed into the window. I looked at the pastor and saw that he was hanging on to the seat for dear life. I asked him what was going on. He said, "I feel like I am going to vomit." I said, "Brother, hanging onto the seat is not going to do you any good. You have paid for this dinner, and you are not going to vomit it. Now because your faith is gone, I am going to pray and you will agree with me." He said, "Alright sister, you pray." I said, "Devil, you have been a prince of the air for a long time. But today I declare that there is another Prince in this air. I command you to stop it in Jesus' name." After repeating that twice, the plane flew straight until we landed in Guatemala. The pastor did not vomit his dinner. It was amazing how the Lord had calmed the wind, and this pastor's stomach, and allowed us to land safely in Guatemala.

How wonderful it was to seek the Lord during the World Congress, with all of us together asking Him for the breakthrough into the nations where the doors were not opening for the gospel. Those nations were in what was then called the 10/40 Window. It was encouraging to hear from people from different parts of the world telling us how God was starting to move in places where the gospel had not been welcomed before. It gave us a glimpse of what the Book of Revelation says about people coming together from every tribe, every tongue, and every nation to praise the name of the Lord.

During the congress, the Lord connected me with a pastor and his wife whom the Lord used to transform the city of Almolonga in Guatemala, mentioned in the Transformation video series by George Otis JR. This pastor had been an idol worshiper, but ended up having a similar conversion to that of Saul of Tarsus (Acts 9:3) on the road as he journeyed from the pub. Then he turned the city from idol worship toward the living God. We were able to go and see for ourselves how the city had been transformed by the power of a miracle-working God. The city actually closed the jail because there was no longer any crime. Cars didn't need to be locked anymore; a purse could be left in the car with windows open, yet no one would touch it. Even the land itself was healed. The crops started yielding enormous fruits and vegetables without fertilizer. One giant carrot could feed a family. The town is now known as the garden of the Americas because the earth is so fertile. Locals said that formerly, the produce was piddling, the jails were full, and drunks stumbled through the streets. Now there's peace and an abundance of fresh produce, and they give the glory to God. The Lord led them to a rock to get water supply for the city. It was an opportunity of a lifetime to spend those few days in the presence of this humble, anointed couple and their leadership. They even booked and paid for a motel room for us so that we could spend time together in the city. Wow! What shall I render to the Lord for all His benefits toward me? I will take up a cup of salvation and call upon the name of the Lord, and I will shout His praises in the presence of all His people.

# UNDER HIS WINGS

## *Taking the City of Mar del Plata, Argentina*

A few months after I went back to Australia, I was invited to help take the city of Mar del Plata, Argentina for Jesus. When Ed Silvoso plans to go into a city, he first gathers the pastors of the city and their congregation to pray. In this city, he had gathered 128 pastors and their congregations to come and pray for their city. That is great unity. When they felt it was the right time to take the city, he invited pastors in the land and from other parts of the world to come and help gather in the harvest. When I arrived, we were assigned a section of the city to focus on. The Lord had given me John 4:38, which says: "I sent you to harvest where you didn't plant. Others have labored and you have entered into their labor." In the morning we had meetings, in the afternoon we went door-to-door dropping off invitations, and in the evening we were bused to our designated area for the meetings. The people were so receptive; in my area we saw many come to the Lord. One night after I had finished preaching and made an altar call, a woman stepped forward and asked me to pray for her twelve-year-old grandson who was born deaf and mute. I commanded the deaf and dumb spirit to leave the boy, and his ears popped open and his tongue was loosed. He was able to speak for the very first time in his life. The very first word out of his mouth was "Hallelujah!" This caused such great joy in that place.

There was a witch who had attended the meeting who was known for giving hell to the Christians who lived around her. When she saw the boy's miracle, she ripped open the top part of her blouse, exposing her upper chest and neck, which was covered with a red, strawberry-like rash. She said to me, "Can you heal me? I have been to many doctors and no one can help me." I said to her, "Lady, you are a witch. But you have seen that my God is more powerful and stronger than your god. Are you willing to renounce your witchcraft and let my God heal you, because He loves you?" She agreed, so I led her in a prayer of repentance and she gave her heart to the Lord. While she stood in front of us, I commanded that rash to leave her body, and her skin was restored back to normal. I did not even touch her. We saw so many other healing in that place. I wish I had more time to tell about everything the Lord did. There were some people whom I prayed for but who were not healed. I don't understand it all, but I made up my mind a long time ago that I am going to continue to trust God in all circumstances and will continue to obey Him by praying for the sick until I see all of them recovered.

CHAPTER 17

# AUSTRALIA-ENGLAND
# RECONCILIATION

The year of 1998 marked the beginning of a busy traveling season for our ministry team. We had a team of intercessors from England meet with the Australian Prayer Network to do reconciliation between the two countries. Some of these British intercessors said they had been praying for 70 years for what was about to happen. That is faithfulness, eh? It reminded me of Daniel praying in Babylon. We traveled all over Australia praying in places where England had committed injustices in connection with the convicts who were being sent to the penal colonies and saw a lot of healing take place. The following year, the Lord said to the Australian Prayer Network leadership, "Now you will take a team to go break the curse and release the blessing over England." When I was asked to be part of the team, I asked the Lord, "Why do I need to go? I do not have the money and I am not aboriginal; my parents were not descendants of the convicts." The English intercessors had already been to Zimbabwe and repented for colonizing my land of birth. When I was in Argentina a friend had purchased a tape recorded by an Englishman, Roger Mitchell, who was the Prayer Network coordinator for Europe and had been one of the speakers when I was there. I had it for six months, but had not listened to it. As I was driving to church asking the Lord why I needed to go to England, the Lord said, "And why have you not listened to Roger Mitchell's tape?" I said, "I don't know why, I just didn't think of it." He said, "You have had it for six months." I said, "Okay, I will listen to it tonight when I get home." Once I had settled into bed that evening, that's just what I did. Ten minutes in, I was on my knees on the floor, travailing for England. Then the Lord said, "That is why I need you to go to England. You are a true intercessor. You will be standing in the gap and not taking sides." I said, "Yes, Lord, I will go." I am glad that I was obedient. The Lord used me in a mighty way.

Upon arriving in England, we were welcomed like royalty. Our first meeting was morning tea with the Queen's Bishop. Security was tight as the Queen's police escorted us. We were ushered into places even where the heads of states don't get to go. We had morning and afternoon meals with mayors of different cities. After the time of reconciliation was over, the Lord opened doors for me to minister for two weeks in different churches. By the time I left England, I had been away from home for a total of eleven weeks!

### Patmos Island

Before going to England, I had been petitioning the Lord for the Island of Patmos. One day my two intercessors, a married couple, said to me, "Deborah, you know how you have always wanted to go to the Island of Patmos? Well, we feel like we are going with you this time." I said, "But you always go with me when you stand in the gap for me and pray." They told me that this time was different and that they felt that the Lord wanted them to be responsible for paying for the whole trip including my visit to Patmos. So when I booked my ticket with the Turkish airlines from Australia to Israel, they threw in a free ticket from Istanbul to Izmir and paid for a taxi from Izmir to Kusadasi. That was unexpected!

One of my intercessor friends joined me on the trip. After spending the night in Kusadasi, we took a boat to Samos, another Greek island, and spent a day and a half there in a beautiful hotel enjoying the delicious Greek food. The next day, we arrived on the island of Patmos. Our hotel shuttle driver was delighted to find out that we were from Australia. He said, "I have waited for 30 years to show kindness to people from Australia. I lived in Australia for 31 years; the people there were so good to me." He told us about how he had to come back to Patmos, the Island of Love, to look after his 91-year-old mother. He gave us his card and told us to call him anytime we needed a ride. My friend and I told him that we would love to go to John the Beloved's cave, where he wrote the book of Revelation. We told him that he could just drop us off and that we would find our own way back to the hotel. We wanted as much time as we needed and not to be rushed. I am glad we did that because when he dropped us off, a bus pulled in with all the prophets and intercessors we had been with at the World Congress in Guatemala. What good timing! We went into the cave to pray together and then went outside to read the entire Book of Revelation together. We prayed together again and the prophets prophesied. During this time, one of the more well known prophets said, "There is a flood coming to India and some of you here will be going there this year after the flood." I thought, "No! Do I have to go to India this year, Lord?" I said that because just before I left Australia, one of the men in our church sat opposite me in the church coffee shop and said, "Deborah, if God ever tells you to go to India, I am ready to pay for your ticket." I responded, "No, give me that money for England and Israel instead. The Lord is sending me to Israel, Turkey, and England this time." He said no and insisted that the money was for me to go to India. When I told him that the Lord had not told me to go to India he simply responded saying, "He will," and we left it at that. Hearing this prophetic word in Patmos began to stir me up about

India. We then traveled with these prophets and intercessors to pray in Ephesus in Turkey for the doors to open for the gospel of Jesus Christ. Wow, Lord! How Your favor crowned the whole trip!

### Canopy of Praise

My friends, John and Annette, and I had been involved in an Australian prayer network called Spirit Alive before it became part of the International Prayer Network. The Lord connected us in Guatemala at the World Congress, where we were representing Australia, and we then participated in the Australia-England reconciliation together. After the England trip, and back in Sydney, we felt a stirring in our hearts for Sydney. So we went to a conference center for a weekend to seek the Lord's heart on the matter. After a time of worship, we went to separate spots to hear from God. While I was alone, God gave me a vision of Jesus skipping on the mountains of Jerusalem. He came in the room at the conference center where we were all sitting down. In His hands, he was holding two pieces of paper. He went around the room trying to pass out these two papers and a pen, but people didn't seem to be taking them from Him. When He got to me, I asked Him, "What are the papers for?" He said to me, "It's a marriage certificate. Whoever wants to get married to Me must sign the paper." I immediately grabbed it and signed it, and then the vision finished. We held a prayer meeting to share what each one heard from the Lord. After that, we felt the time was right to have a time of ministry in Sydney to worship the King of glory as a city. We found a venue in West Ryde, which is a central location in the city and is accessible and easy for people to reach by public transportation. John and Annette, who are beautiful worship leaders, were in charge of leading the worship and my part was to lead intercession. People came from all over Sydney. We met once a month, we worshipped up to five and half hours at a time, only stopping when God gave a prophetic word or a Scripture to be read.

It's amazing how quickly time goes when you are in the presence of the Lord. Even after five hours, people didn't want to leave. It was awesome!

I was at the second World Congress when the Lord called me to go to Spain. Not knowing how to break the news to John and Annette, I felt the Lord telling me to invite them over for dinner, so I did. Unbeknownst to me, the Lord had called them to go to the mission field too, so in the meantime they were also thinking, "How are we going to break the news to Deborah?" After dinner I said, "I have something to tell you, but I don't know where to start or how to say it." They said, "We were also wondering how we were going to tell you the news we have." It then became easy to talk about it and to work out how to let people know about what God had called us to do. John and Annette were called to go to England and I was called to go to Spain. I am glad to say John and Annette are now back in Australia. They built a wonderful Worship Center in New South Wales on a place higher than the clouds where ministry teams can stay for a time. When you are there you feel like you are sitting in a plane; it's beautiful.

# CHAPTER 18

# INDIA AND THE PHILIPPINES

*India*

After I returned from England in November 1999, I had only two and a half weeks to prepare for India. We had a good-sized team, the majority of whom were young, except for the pastor from our church (Pastor Graham), his wife, and me. The team had already been meeting and praying together, so when I arrived, the team said, "The Lord said we can't go without you." The man who had previously spoken with me about India approached me and said, "Deborah, I am ready to pay. How much is the trip?" I told him the total and he promised that he would bring it to me the next day. He even gave me spending money. He and his wife were excited to be part of what God was going to do on that mission trip.

I knew that where we were going in India, women did not preach in church, so I was preparing messages to teach in the Bible school and in women's ministries. But Pastor Graham said to me, "Deborah, prepare to preach your messages." I said to him, "But women are not allowed to preach in India." He said, "You never know what the Lord will do, so be prepared to preach in the churches as well." We traveled to South India, which is very beautiful with all of its beaches. The Lord even gave me the opportunity to ride an elephant! We were going to be working with a pastor who oversaw over 500 churches that had been born out of his ministry. They also had a Bible school on the grounds with classes and dormitories for both men and women, but in separate buildings so that males and females didn't sit in the same class. In that culture, they do everything separately. Even in church, the men sit on one side and the women on the other.

We would teach during the day and, after showering and eating dinner, we would spend time worshiping and soaking in prayer, getting filled up in order to give away what we had freely received. What we had to give was eagerly received by the people there, who were hungry, very friendly and receptive. Every night, we were taken to a different church. There was such unity among the pastors; they were so hungry for the presence of God. One night, back at the house, we were brushing our teeth and getting ready to go when there was a knock on our door. I opened it to find Pastor Graham standing there. He said, "Deborah, you are on tonight, not me." I said, "Pastor Graham! I only have ten minutes before we get picked up." He said, "I did tell you to prepare before we left Australia, so there you are. Tonight, you're on."

I grabbed one of my messages right before we were picked up. At the church, the locals lead us in worship first before allowing our team to lead. Next, the local pastor introduced the speaker, whom he thought would be Pastor Graham. Pastor Graham took the microphone and introduced our team. He then asked if anyone there had a problem with a woman preaching. They all answered, "No." He asked three times, and three times they said, "No." Then he said, "Since no one has a problem with a woman preacher, tonight we will hear from a powerful woman of God who is also one of the preachers in our church. Deborah, come." He gave me the microphone and sat down. They asked the senior pastor's wife to be my translator. I preached on "the fire must be kept burning" from Leviticus 6:12-13 and the fire did fall in that place. During ministry time, men were asked to lay hands on men to pray and women on women. But when the men saw what was happening in the women's section, they all crammed into the women's section to get me to lay hands on them for impartation. They were all so hungry. We saw God do amazing things through many healings.

The last week we were there, we did an open-air service. We saw people saved, healed, and baptized in the Holy Spirit; it was awesome! We were going to have another open-air two nights before we left, but as we were worshiping and praying, we all felt we should not go and ended up cancelling the service. That very night, lightning struck right on the spot where we would have been. That lightning demolished half of the brick wall, a tree, a table, and even struck the wife of the man who owned the place, though she survived. How wonderful is our God. If we had had the meeting, more people would have been hurt and maybe even killed. We were so grateful for the warning of the Holy Spirit. The last meeting was a gathering of pastors and leaders, who, after the meeting ended, all took off their Sunday best and put on servant's clothing. They lined their people up and laid banana leaves in front of them. One pastor in the front served rice and one followed with meat and vegetables. They did that until everyone was fed, including the children, not eating until everything had been cleaned up. Wow! They modeled humility for us beautifully. The Lord truly blessed our time there.

### The Philippines

In 2000, we went and visited Mindanao, the southernmost island of the Philippines. We had a bigger team, consisting of both mature adults and youth. It was not a safe place for us to visit at that time; some radical Muslims had already killed one Australian missionary and taken some other missionaries hostage and were threatening to kill them all. This all started happening just after we booked our tickets to go on a mission trip there. Our government said, "No one is to go there. If you do, you go at your own risk." We prayed as a team and individually, but no one felt to pull out. The travel agent with whom we booked our tickets offered to refund the money if we decided not to go. But we all felt that it was the right time and that the Lord wanted us to go. We had to sign a form saying, "If I don't come back, I take full responsibility." While we were there, we could not tell who was a real soldier and who was not. We had heard that some radicals would kill the soldiers and take their guns and put on their uniforms. So every time we needed to go to the shops, we went in groups with the locals. Despite the danger, God was so gracious to us. We went to different cities and saw many people saved, healed, delivered, and baptized in the Holy Spirit.

In one of the cities, God gave us favor with the mayor, who had been saved on his deathbed in hospital in Manila (though his wife was not yet saved). He had Scriptures written all over the city, even in parks. When he heard about us, he invited us to afternoon tea. He sent out all his staff because he wanted to be alone with us and served us himself. He gave us the town hall so we could hold our meetings there. One night while we were worshiping, the Lord set the building on fire. He had done it twice before in Sydney, but here in the Philippines, people gathered outside watching the building on fire and wondered how we could still be singing in there. Somebody called the firemen. We were not aware of it until they walked in and told us to get out of the building because it was on fire. They went up and searched for the fire, but could not find any. When we went out, we noticed the people around the building watching the fire. When the firemen could not find the fire, they told us we could go back in and all those people who had been watching the fire came in. On that night, 119 people gave their lives to the Lord, including the mayor's wife.

The mayor was so happy that he booked us into a beautiful resort at his own expense. We continued to see many healings and miracles over the next two weeks. On the two Sundays that we were there, we realized that there were more churches to minister to than we could cover with the number of people on our team. So the churches changed their service times so that we could minister to them all, traveling from one to the next and the next.

One of the miracles that stand out to me was that of a woman who was paralyzed on one side. I had been praying for the sick at the front of the church when a lady came and said, "Will you pray for my mother?" I said, "Sure, which one is your mother?" thinking she was one of those waiting in front. But she grabbed my hand and dragged me instead to the back row of seats. When I got there, there was her mother, paralyzed on one side. When I saw her condition, I thought to myself, "Do I have faith for this?" But I quickly remembered that my business is to pray and God's is to heal. So I knelt beside the lady and said, "Mama, do you mind if I put my hands on your knee and pray?" She said, "No, I don't mind at all." I put my hands on her knee and commanded death to leave and life to come back. I declared that she would receive restoration. Her leg and her arm then shot up and shook like a reed. When the shaking stopped, I asked her to do something. She stood up and walked up and down. The place immediately went crazy and the faith level of people increased. Miracles started breaking out everywhere. Thank you, Jesus, for showing up and showing off.

# CHAPTER 19

# SECOND WORLD CONGRESS: GUATEMALA, 2000

If you are willing and obedient, you will eat the fruit of the land. Before we went to the World Congress in 2000, we had a national prayer conference. I was very privileged to be asked to open that conference in prayer, after which I was invited again to represent Australia at the World Congress. The Congress was to be held in a Sheraton, which is a huge, beautiful hotel, but it was also quite expensive. Finances were still tight at the time, but the Lord made a way for me to be there. Two other ladies whom I was close to had also been invited but, like me, did not have a lot of money to spend. So we agreed to share a room in the hotel.

The morning that we arrived, we were ushered to our room that had three beds. Before I unpacked, however, the hotel phone rang. I picked it up and found myself speaking with a gentleman from the front desk. "Can I speak to Deborah Williams, please?" I said, "Speaking." He said, "There has been a big mistake. Would you mind coming down to the front desk, please?" I went down and the gentleman at the front desk started to apologize, saying that they had made a big mistake and that I had been taken to the wrong room. Apparently, I had been booked in an executive suite. I tried to convince them that I could not pay for an executive suite, but it was like I was speaking a foreign language; they would not hear me. They kept apologizing and saying, "We will take you to look at the room and if you are not happy with it, we will take you to another one." I said, "I can't pay for an executive suite," but they said, "It's already been paid for." I don't know how it was paid for, but it was sure nice to be spoiled. Later I found that the Lord had given me this suite so that I would be able to pray for high-profile people in there.

It was in that Congress that God called me to go to Spain as a long-term missionary. At first, I cried buckets and told the Lord that He should send a white person. He could send someone who knew the language. I didn't have any money and still had a mortgage on my house. But He would not accept any of my excuses. Everywhere I went, Spain would come up or I would be confronted with something to do with Spain. Then the Lord said, "Deborah, are you willing to go for a thousand tongues to sing my Redeemer's praise?" When I said, "Yes, Lord, I will go," I was filled with tremendous peace, even though I still didn't have the money. I would have to sell my car and get a tenant so that I could rent out my house. But the Lord was able to make everything come together for me so that I could go.

I worked up until two days before I left. On the morning after my last shift, after I had my quiet time and finished my devotions, I said, "Daddy, I need a laptop to be able to communicate with my family. I have never used a computer before, so I am asking for one like my son-in-law's [George], so he can teach me how to send emails. Thank You, Daddy, for my laptop. Amen." I went to put my head on the pillow to sleep, then the phone rang. "Deborah, my name is Dawn. I believe you are praying for a laptop and I believe we are supposed to provide you with the money for the laptop. So can you give me your account number? I will deposit the money into your account and you can go and choose the laptop you want." Wow!

When we busy ourselves with His business, He busies Himself with our business.

I rang my friend Margaret who worked in the place where they sold laptops. In those days, you had to order first before you could buy one. But God had made a way for me! When Margaret answered my call, she said, "Let me ask my boss. There is one extra laptop that was sent today with the order we received. But I can't buy it for you on my staff discount." I said, "No, I am not asking you to buy in your name. I will pay what they are asking for." She went and talked to her boss, who was not a believer, and mentioned that I was going to be a missionary. Her boss said, "Missionaries do a good job. I will give it to her for the cost price." WOW! That was better than the staff discount. I picked it up and went to George and Hazel's house so that George could give me a quick lesson on how to send emails.

I was finally ready for the big adventure. When facing intimidating circumstances, it is important to keep reminding myself that I am in Christ, no matter where I am, and that He will not let me down. Oh, give thanks to the Lord, for He is good. His mercy endures forever. Oh, give thanks to the Lord, for His goodness to the sons of men. Oh! That men would give thanks to the Lord!

CHAPTER 20

# GOING WITHOUT KNOWING
# WHERE I WAS GOING

With my ticket, my laptop, my suitcase and twenty American dollars in my pocket, I got on a plane to go to a country that I had never been to, where I didn't speak the language, but I knew that God was with me. I was on an adventure of a lifetime.

Two days after I arrived, I was invited to go to a pastors' conference in a nearby hotel. Cindy Jacobs had previously committed to going to Spain once a year for ten years; this was her fifth year. Before the meeting started, I went into the hotel's conference room to pray. A brother from the Dominican Republic also came in to pray and asked if he could pray for me. Then he said, "Actually, I have a word for you. Can I give it to you?" I said, "Yes, please." Then he said, "The Lord is saying He wants to bless you tonight. So when you are called to stand up, do not be embarrassed to stand up." I thanked him and we continued to pray for the meeting.

Cindy was the last speaker. When she finished preaching, she said to me, "Sister, stand up!" Then she turned to the pastors, "This is to all you pastors and leaders here. The Lord is saying, 'You have money in your pockets American dollars, not pesetas. Come and give it to this sister. She has left her country to serve in your nation. Come now and bless her.'" I felt like I was enveloped in the Father's love, which felt like a warm blanket. I was standing with my eyes closed, weeping as they came and gave me their money. I left that conference with $1,669. WOW! God is full of untold surprises. That was my first provision from the Lord in Spain.

When I first arrived in Spain, I began my work by ministering to drug addicts. The church had a drug rehabilitation center, where I spent sleepless nights praying with those who were going through withdrawals. I knew I was royal in my identity, but I chose to act as a servant. Before the powers of darkness, I was a ruler and gave no room for their influence. Jesus is our example; He is the King of kings, yet a servant of all.

The first thing I did in the church was to establish a prayer meeting. The enemy cannot beat down those with strong prayer lives. They may get knocked down, but they will get up again. Because the church was in an industrial area, people would stop by the prayer meeting at 6:00 AM while on their way to work. The group grew stronger as more and more people were getting delivered. The word got out to the workers in the factories. They started coming and knocking on the church doors, saying, "Can I come in for prayer? I heard that you pray for people to be freed from demons and addictions." Many people were saved and delivered and then began bringing their families to church too. And so the church began to grow.

From South America, I had learned the secret of motivating people to grow in the Lord after they got saved. After people were saved, I would take them through classes to understand what had happened to them. Once they discovered who they were in Christ, then we would take them away for a weekend of divine encounter, breaking off all bondages and curses.

While I was ministering during a divine encounter, one of the ladies at the divine encounter started to hiss at me like a snake. She turned a blue color, like a lizard, and, with her tongue out and fingernails all curled up, she said, "I will kill you." All the ladies were terrified, including the leaders. They had never seen anything like this. They were relieved when I cast the demons out of her and she became normal again. After she was set free, the rest of the ladies were able to relax and receive God's love, having seen such an incredible demonstration. However, there was one woman still bound. I said, "Lord, if this lady goes away bound up, I will have failed. Please show me what to do." I felt that the Lord said, "Call her out and pray for her." I did, and she fell down. When I knelt beside her, then I sensed that I should put my hand on her stomach and command rejection to leave her. She let out a piercing scream and was set free. It was like an egg had just been cracked open. I asked her what happened when she was in the womb. She told me that her parents didn't want a baby when they found out they were pregnant. She herself had a husband who loved her dearly; they had two wonderful sons and a successful Italian shoe shop. But she was miserable and could not receive love. God in His mercy set her free. Out of this experience, I learned how to focus on the one in front of me. At the end of our session, they had all had an encounter with the Lord and were filled with the Holy Spirit. We all left celebrating the goodness of our God.

We did this with everyone who got saved. They would come back on Sunday afternoon from their weekends away and would get water baptized that evening. They would invite their families and friends to come to the baptism. Out of this, we saw families come to the Lord once they had seen the changes being made in their family members. People would call the office and say, "I want to see the woman who changed my husband/wife/daughter/son," depending on which member of the family it was. Some were saved at the baptism services. During one encounter weekend, there was a lady with us who had been separated from her husband for a year, and although they lived under the same roof, they did not talk to each other. She received ministry that weekend and was set free on Saturday night. Early Sunday morning, her husband, who had not spoken to her for a whole year, called her to apologize, wanting to be given another chance. He had not spoken to her for a whole year and now he could not wait for her to come home. He said that he didn't know what had got into him. It turns out that when she was set free, he was also set free at home. He offered to pick her up and take her to church for baptism, where he got saved too.

We saw marriages and families healed and restored. Isn't that just like God? The very thing the enemy destroyed in my own life was now what God was using me to restore. It brings tears to my eyes even as I write it. It's true that God works out all things for our good for us, we who love Him, if we don't give up.

At the time that I arrived in Spain, it was spiritually dark. In some towns, there was not a single believer. At certain times of the year, streets are actually lined up with flags to honoring the devil. The darkness was so thick in some places that you felt like you could cut it with a knife. One day someone said, "Did you know that Spain is known as a cemetery for missionaries?" I said, "Thank you for telling me, but Spain is not going to be a cemetery for this missionary. I am not in Spain, I am in Christ." She agreed. But even then, I could see that the enemy was trying to make me leave Spain. My daughter in Australia had fallen on a wet floor in a supermarket and hurt her back. She could not pick up her own baby. But she said, "Mum, don't come back; we are managing." Thankfully, God provided foster mothers to help my daughter and husband when he had to go to work. The enemy continued to fight against me using any means he could find. For example, every night there would be a congregation of over a dozen cats making haunting noises below my window from 1:00 to 2:30 AM. One night, I got fed up and commanded them to leave and never come back. One night I got tired of it. I filled a bucket with hot water, opened the window, and threw the water on them. That was the end of my disturbed sleep.

To continue being effective, I spent a lot of time in the presence of God, in worship and prayer, and in the Word, getting drunk in the Spirit. Intimacy with the Lord is my source for all I need. I knew that it was of the uttermost importance for me to be sustained while in Spain.

My neighbors used to love coming to watch me whenever they heard me laughing. My apartment was above my landlord's house. I would leave the door slightly open, and the joy would spread. Some people would be set free from all kinds of bondages by being in the presence of God. There seems to be extra grace when you are on the mission field, to keep you going or to carry you through the hardships that you don't understand.

One morning, I was praying for a sick man. At that time I could not speak much Spanish at all and was still learning the difference between masculine and feminine words; there are masculine words for male and feminine words for female. As I was praying for this particular man, I thought I was saying, "Heal your son, Lord," but in Spanish, I was actually saying, "Heal your daughter, Lord!" The Lord was gracious and healed him anyway, after everyone burst into laughter. The following week I prayed for a lady who was paralyzed and found out later that I was calling her God's "son." I was commanding resurrection life to come into her, but in Spanish I was saying "into him." Resurrection life came into her anyway and she was completely healed. Praise His wonderful name. Even when we are making mistakes with words, if there is love in our hearts, He still comes and does what He does best. I am so thankful that He is always there to heal, even when we mess it up.

One day, I was standing outside talking to one of the ladies. A man got in his car parked out in front and began to drive off. The lady suddenly realized that her two-year-old daughter was not near her and said, "Where is my baby?" The next moment, she let out a loud scream. The baby had been run over. I ran and picked up the baby, but she was dead. I put her against my chest and started to command death to leave and life to come back into her body. I also prayed for restoration, that there would be no reminder of the devil's work. The baby came back to life and miraculously; there was not a mark on her. I called back the mother, who was still wailing.

We hugged and celebrated the goodness of God. It all happened so quickly. I was in shock. I had no time to think or let doubt creep in. I was not able to talk about it for eight years, but it took my faith to another level.

One Sunday, the pastor and his wife were away so I again preached on "the fire must be kept burning" out of Leviticus 6:9,12-13. As I preached, the fire fell. I did not make an altar call but stood in the front still holding the microphone. One by one, men and women started coming to the front, confessing their sins publicly. It was like the fire of God had laid bare what was in the hearts of the people. The service started at 10:00 AM, at 2:00 PM we were still there. God had visited His people. When the pastor and his wife came back, the congregation was telling them to listen to the tape of the service. His wife said, "I don't know if I am ready for it." But whenever a pastor from another church would visit the office, our pastor would always say, "If you want fire in your church, invite this sister."

We saw God doing amazing things and the Lord continued to open doors for me and grant me favor. It was hard work, but I loved every minute. I used to prepare the lessons and my messages in English, and then translate everything into Spanish. I even had to do that with the songs as well. I was burning the candle at both ends; you can imagine how much work was involved.

### Praying for the Nations

As I mentioned before, we had a prayer meeting every morning. We had flags of different nations on the walls. After praying for Spain, we would bring down whichever flag the Lord was highlighting to us and would pray for that nation.

On one occasion, as soon as we walked into the building, the Lord said to me, "Get the American flag, lay it down, and get everyone to come and kneel on it and pray for America." I said, "Lord,

America already has so many Christians. They should be praying for us." The Lord said, "Deborah, pray for America." I have learned to tell when it's an urgent command and to obey by praying. Later, I came to find out why. As we were praying, I went into a deep travail. We were weeping before the Lord, not knowing what it was about. This all took place on September 11, 2001. Later that afternoon, one of my people came running to my apartment. She had just heard the news and said, "Deborah, this is why the Lord had us praying! Terrorists have attacked America." So we continued to pray for the families affected and hoped that some lives were spared.

One of the main issues we continually faced in Spain was the slavery to drugs. Some families would send their sons to sell drugs. When the sons were caught and sent to jail, they would serve their time and then return to their families, who would then send them out to sell drugs again. It was a vicious circle. The ministry I worked with, as I mentioned before, had a rehabilitation center. The authorities trusted the center and would release prisoners to serve their time here, after which we would help them find jobs. We had quarters for men, women, and families. Whenever someone had a birthday, we made a fuss and did whatever we could to make them feel loved and special. We were their family.

One young man stands out in my memory. He was 18 years old and a very nice kid. His grandma, who was 73 years old, came for his birthday from another town, even though she was only there three hours at the most. After two weeks she called the office to talk to me, but I was out. She wanted to know if I was okay because the Lord had been telling her to pray for me day and night. I told the girls in the office, "If she calls again and I am out, please tell her to keep praying." The Lord knows why I need prayer even though I may not.

I received an invitation to go to Hanover, a city in Germany, to a gathering of 61 nations to seek the Lord for Europe. We gathered to summon Europe to worship the King of kings and Lord of lords. At the time, Europe was very dark and resistant to the gospel.

When I was there, the grandma called again so the girls in the office told her to keep praying. At the last session of that gathering, Cindy Jacobs was the speaker. When she finished, she pointed at me and said, "Sister, the Lord is saying, 'You have the key to Europe.' Come up and lead us in prayer." She then pointed to an African brother who was also a missionary in Europe and said to him, "You too, come and pray." We prayed and the meeting finished. We went back to Spain with the prayer network leaders, Peter Wagner and Cindy Jacobs. First, we prayed in Madrid, Spain, the only city that has a statue of Satan.

We left Madrid that evening and journeyed to the city where I was working. Three times the Lord said to me, "Change cars!" I told this to the driver, who was the personal assistant to the pastor with whom I was working. She said, "Please, Deborah, stay with us and pray." I didn't want to dishonor her in front of those who worked under her, so I stayed. But when we stopped for gas, the pastor's son who had been traveling with us decided to change cars.

Around 4:00 AM, we had a terrible car accident. Our car hit the guardrail and flew in the air like in a movie and landed on its roof. The locals were thrown out of the car, but I was trapped inside. I knew I had broken bones. The fuel tank had ruptured and saturated me with gas, soaking my whole body. My eyes were drowning in it and burning. I knew at any minute the car could burst into flames. I said, "Lord, You promised, 'When we go through the fire we will not be burned.' Please don't let this car burst into flames." Hot water from the cracked radiator started to burn me. "Lord, I don't know what You are going to do with this water. Please don't let it burn me." All of a sudden the hot water stopped dripping and did not burn me. Every breath I could master was a prayer. I knew that if I stopped praying I would die. The pain was indescribable. I have had three children, but the pain I endured in that car accident was worse than childbirth. My body was covered with cuts from the broken glass. I started to declare, "These bones are not dry. You restored bones in Ezekiel's Valley (Ezekiel 37: 4-10). Lord, you can restore these bones." I said, "Lord, my children released me to come and do Your will. Don't let the enemy take my life. What will it do to their faith if they have to be called to come and get my body?" I repeated my declarations, saying again and again, "These bones are not dry, Lord, I know You are able to restore me. I will not die; I will live to declare the goodness of the Lord in the land of the living (Psalm 27:13, 118:17)." While I did that, a young missionary from the US started declaring the same thing outside the car, not knowing that that was what I was declaring inside the car. The time I spent in that car boosted my faith to a whole new level. Despite what was happening, I knew I was not going to die. Though death stared me in the face and I was close to slipping into its dark shadows. I cried out to the Lord, God came and saved me. He was so kind, so gracious to me! Because of His passion toward me, He made everything right and He restored me! So I have learned from my experience, that God protects His children. I was broken and brought low. He answered me and came to my rescue. Now I can say to myself and to all, relax and rest, be confident for the Lord rewards fully those who trust in Him! God rescued my soul from death's fear and dried up my eyes of many tears. He kept my feet firmly on the path, and strengthened me so that I may live my life before Him in His life giving light

The ambulance in Spain took so long to come. The police came before them and said, "This is a miracle. We have never seen a person come out of this kind of accident alive. Normally the car bursts into flames. Someone up there is looking after you." They cut the wreckage and got me out. I was cut all over by broken glass. Eventually the ambulance came and took me to the hospital. The x-rays kept changing as the team was praying for me. The doctors told me that, I would not be able to walk again and that my right shoulder was minced and my lower back discs were crushed, but I rejected their diagnoses. Before I was flown back to Australia, I asked to be put in a wheelchair and be taken to the church. When we got there, I asked to be wheeled close to the pulpit. Touching the pulpit, I made a declaration. I said, "Church, I am going home to be healed. I will

be back, I will stand on this same pulpit and preach the gospel again"
Before I left Spain, I said to the devil, "If you want a fight, you have
got one, one of us is going to lose and it's not going to be me. I am
going home to be healed. I will be back to preach the gospel. You are
going to watch me walk and dance before the Lord with both hands
lifted up". So I was flown back to Australia. My family came to pick
me up from the airport. When my grandson Joel Daniel saw me in
a wheelchair, he would not come near me.

I later found out that before the accident he had made a
paper plane. When his parents asked him what he was making, he
said, "I am making a plane to go and get my Gammy. Who is looking after her over there?" So when I arrived home in a wheelchair,
he felt responsible, like he had failed to look after his Gammy. He
would not come near me. It took a while to convince him that he was
not responsible and I was going to get better and walk again. I told
him to pray for Gammy to be healed and be able to walk again. My
daughter Hazel had to shower me, clothe me, and comb my hair. I
had not been able to lie down because my shoulder blade was stick-
ing out like a coat hanger and the discs in my back were crushed.
Hazel took me to the doctor in Australia. He gave the same negative
report, but I told him that I was going to be healed and go back to
the mission field.

The next Sunday, I asked them to take me to church. When
I was being prayed for at church, I did not tell them that I could not
lie down. I said to the Lord, pointing to the carpet, "This is Your
operating table. You are my only hope. I am not leaving this carpet
until You are finished with me." The service went on until my healing was completed. When I felt He was done with me, I went to get
up. People rushed to help me. I said, "Please don't touch me. I have
something to do first." I lifted both arms to the Lord and thanked
Him for the creative miracle He had done for me by giving me a
new shoulder and new discs in my spine. Then I said, "Devil, do you
remember what I said? Look, I have two hands lifted up praising my
God."

After I was healed and before returning to Spain, I was advised that I needed to register my worldwide evangelistic activities as a ministry and to see a particular accountant. He was a successful man who looked after very big ministries and told me that he could not look after my ministry because he was too busy. I accepted this and left. But after I left, the Lord spoke to this man and told him that He wanted him to look after me. So before I got home, he called me and told me to come back because he wanted to obey the Lord. He did help me and eventually I got my ministry registered as *Under His Wings*. He introduced me to a businessman who felt that if my ministry was insured under him, it would be less expensive. I agreed and met with both of them. The two of them and three other friends became board members.

I went to Spain knowing that the Lord wanted me to be there for five years. The enemy does not care how you start, but he surely cares how you finish. In my fourth year before I went back for the Christmas holidays, the businessman came to see the work I was doing in Spain. He was very happy with what he saw. I even got him opportunities to minister there. But when he returned to Australia, he organized his own ministries with the plan that when I returned for Christmas break, I would not go back to Spain, but go to Fiji and Samoa, where he planned for me to run the Bible schools he wanted to start. I told him that I had one more year, and then, if that is what the Lord would want me to do, I would do it. He said, "If you want our support, you have to forget about Spain. We will give you a house, a car, and money if you agree to run our ministries." I said, "I am sorry, but I can't allow money to control the call of God on my life." He said, "Do you know that you only have 27 cents in your account?" I said, "Yes, I do." He said, "If you go to Spain, you go on your own with 27 cents." I said, "That will have to do. All I know is that I need to complete the five years. I am grateful for what you have done for me." He was not very happy, but we parted on otherwise good terms.

Thank goodness, I had my ticket already. I remembered the

words of Jesus when He sent the 72 in Luke 10:4: "Carry no money-bags." Then, in verse 18, "Behold, I have given you authority over all the power of the enemy and nothing shall hurt you," and in verse 20, "Rejoice that your name is written in heaven." Right there I knew that I had all that I needed. I was joyful to be able to go. I thought to myself, "I am not just going to be in Spain but I am in Christ. I have experienced His compassion, how can I not go? I love Jesus because He first loved me." In Job 23:10, Job said, "He knows the way that I take, when He has tested me, I will come forth like gold." First Peter 1:7 says, "This test is necessary so that your faith may be found genuine, even though it is tested by fire, and may result in praise, glory and honor at the revelation of Jesus Christ."

To this businessman, it was just about money. But to me, God had put a burden on my heart; I was not motivated by their money but by the passion God had put in my heart to see the kingdom expanded. I was in a situation where I had to ask myself, "Am I going to let money control the vision God has put in my heart?" It takes passion to pursue a vision. I decided that the same God who had been faithful to provide for me when I arrived with twenty dollars was going to be faithful with 27 cents. Obedience and a passion for the will of God to be done in my life were my motivations, and I had already paid the price. I made sure my heart was right with those who had been the board of directors. Then I prayed, "Lord, I will speak of what You have done. I remember how far you have carried me. You have never given up on me. You are faithful to the end. Your love is always chasing me. Your kindness is overwhelming and Your hope for me unending. All of my life Your love has been true. You are faithful and Your love is my great defender. I know You will never let me down. I am confident of this: You go before me, Defender of my heart. You make a way where there is no way."

So there I was in Spain with 27 cents in my account, not knowing what to do. The board members kept the mailing list of my financial supporters I had recruited before I came under their insurance. You could say it was betrayal. But I chose not to allow that to be a hindrance to my relationships and continued to walk in love and forgiveness. I knew that was important for my relationship with the Lord and for my success on the mission field.

I had no idea how I was going to get back to my town because it was 45 minutes away from Barcelona airport, but I had peace in my heart. Praise God, when I arrived, my landlords were already at the airport. In the car on the way home, the wife said, "We are going to take you to our home first and have some lunch. We would like to talk with you." I thought, I hope they are not planning to put the rent up; I only have 27 cents to my name. I have less than when I first came! But I still trust You, Lord." After lunch they said, "While you were in Australia, we decided that we don't want you to have to pay rent, electricity, or gas. Your payment will be to pray for our family. We knew you would be tired when you came back, so we filled your fridge and freezer with food. That should last you for a while." In that part of Spain, most families have organic "hobby" farms that are passed on for generations. Someone would always come and say, "I was at the farm to pick fruit, veggies, and eggs for my family and brought a box for you, too." Someone else would come and say, "I was at the butcher buying meat for my family, so I bought you some too." The butchers in Spain cut off all the fat from the meat and cut the meat how you would like it. One box would fill my entire freezer. That is how I survived that year.

One by one, I began contacting my supporters. I needed some prayer backup. So my faithful friend Riina Stefas, talked to her son Tony, who offered to look after the newsletters. Oh, how I am grateful for faithful friends like Russell and Debra Oslington who supported me till the end of my tough times even after I completed the mission. Only the Lord knows how grateful I am for them. They have come to the rescue many times over the years. By the Lord's provision, I was able to minister in other countries from my European base in Spain. Faithfully, I completed my assignment in Spain. Those who trust in the Lord will never be put to shame.

When I went back to Australia, I learned that one of the

board members who had left me with only 27 cents was being treated for an aggressive brain tumor. There was not much time between when they diagnosed him and the time of his death. It was very sad to watch such an intelligent man reduced to a state where he could not do things for himself. His wife was not being very nice to him; she would just put a jug of water by his bed and then leave for the day. I offered to look after him daily, even after he was taken to palliative care. I sat beside his bed in the hospital until he passed. Life is so short; we can't afford to waste it. Let us use it for His glory.

A while after I came back from the mission field, I started having a lot of pain in my back, so the doctor sent me for some tests. Soon after, he decided to send me for a bone density scan. The test result showed that I had osteoporosis. When the doctor put me on medication, I read about the side effects and decided not to take them, choosing instead to pray. After praying for a while, I asked the doctor to send me back for another bone density test. He said, "Deborah, there wouldn't be a change in such a short time like this." I said, "Please, doctor, I am feeling better. I don't want to take the tablets. I have been praying, and I know that there has been a change." He said, "How do you know there is a change?" I said, "Please, doctor." So he wrote me a referral for another test and I made an appointment. While I was waiting for the date of the appointment to come, I went to Pastor Bernadette's Friday prophetic prayer meeting. A seer told me, "Deborah, I have just seen the Lord giving you new bones." She didn't know about the osteoporosis diagnosis, which is how I knew that this was a confirmation that I didn't need to take the tablets. And it was good to have it confirmed with another test, showing that I had been healed. I am so grateful to the Lord for His love, mercy, and goodness to me. If it were not for the Lord, I would have died a long time ago. Oh, the power of the name of Jesus! I will shout it out!

# CHAPTER 21

# AFRICA-EUROPE
# RECONCILIATION

While I was still in Spain, more doors started to open for me to go and minister in other parts of Europe, such as Germany, Portugal, and Poland, to mention a few. Some of these nations I have been to more than once. When God wants to use you, He will find you. I was in a very small town in Spain when the World Prayer Network coordinator of England contacted me. These European spiritual leaders had already gone to Africa and repented for colonizing the countries there. Then they were led to Lagos in Portugal, which is the gateway into Europe where the slave market was built after the gathering at the round table in Berlin between 1884-1885; the objective was to divide Africa and take out the wealth of those countries.

The prayer coordinator of England thus contacted me in Spain and asked me if I would go to Portugal to represent the women of Africa when they gathered there. He knew me from the Australia-England reconciliation and World Congresses. So we met in Lagos in 2004, where the European leaders repented before all of us who were there from Africa. Then the Lord directed them to do a prophetic act. They were to hire a boat (by the way, the owner of the boat would not take any money) and take us all out to sea. Upon returning, we were welcomed back to shore as ministers of the gospel into Europe. Reconciliation and the exchange of gifts were done on the dry, sandy beach facing the old slave market building that still stands there. A funny thing happened: as soon as we left the beach, the waves almost immediately covered the place where we had been standing, as if the Lord had added a seal of approval. Before we went back to the countries from where we had come, the European leaders felt the Lord wanted us to gather in Berlin, where the round table gathering had taken place, and have us Africans pray to break the curse and release blessing over Europe. So the following year in 2005, we gathered in Berlin and prayed over Europe. We felt the curse break and that the Father's blessing had at last been released into the continent.

After I went back to Spain, the Spanish spiritual leaders felt it was time to do reconciliation with Portugal before we gathered in Berlin. So we went back to Lagos before heading to Berlin. To my surprise, when we went back to Lagos, the Lord had healed that city, which had once been so poor. The shops were flourishing. It's true when the people turn from their wicked ways and pray, God hears them from heaven and He heals their land.

After Portugal, I was compelled to gather the Spanish leaders to go to the All Nations Convocation and do reconciliation with Israel for the massacre of the Jews during the Inquisition. The leaders felt it was right and so we went and saw much healing that took place in Israel.

During the All Nations Convocation in Israel, I was chosen to be part of the team of prophetic intercessors who were sent to pray in strategic places throughout Israel. We spent a couple of afternoons with cabinet ministers and prayed in many influential places. We prayed in the place where they train the Rabbis, in a hospital, and even in some places that I cannot write about. But I am glad to let you know that one of the places that we went into was Father Abraham's house in Hebron that is over 3,000 years old. Underneath is the cave where he and Sarah, Isaac and Rebekah, and Jacob and Leah were buried. We were also able to go inside where the Golden Gate is sealed on the Temple Mount in Jerusalem, where the King of glory is going to come through. Soon after we prayed in there, the Muslims closed this area to the public. Wow, Lord what a privilege for little me! It reminded me of when the Lord led me to climb Ayers Rock in Australia and declare some things up there. The very next day the Aboriginal brothers closed it as a sacred site. No one is allowed to climb it anymore. It was a miracle for someone like me who had had a fear of heights to begin with, to climb to the top.

While I was still in Spain, there was a lady, Maria, in the church who had had a hard life. She had been widowed young and left with five children to raise by herself. But I could see her potential; she was so hungry for God. She was teachable and willing to learn. Every morning at 8:00 AM, she would be at my door before she went to work. She would say, "Deborah, I don't know how long the Lord will have you here, and I would like to learn as much as I can while I can." So I took her under my wing and mentored her. She was a lovely lady and was quick to learn. She became so good at doing what I was doing that she ended up traveling with me and ministering with me. By the time I was about to leave, she was able to run the divine encounters, virtually doing what I had been doing. I even brought her to Australia and had her travel and minister with me.

## Papua New Guinea

I was invited to connect Spanish people with the spiritual leaders in Papua New Guinea to do reconciliation between the two nations, because of the massacre of the New Guineans by the Spanish people 400 years ago. Wow, I don't know how God always gets me to do these things I never knew about. Anyway, by His grace, we went. I was scheduled to minister to pastors and leaders gathered in Port Moresby before the elections. They desired that before leaving office, the outgoing Prime Minister would change some of the laws that he had put in place, but were not good for the people or for the country. By God's grace, things shifted and changes were made after we prayed.

When ministering in churches there, we learned to expect the unexpected. Some people come to church with machetes in their hands! (It is important to stay close to the leaders who invite you to their churches and not wander away on your own.) We were booked on a boat to go down to Mailu Island in Mega Land, where a massacre had taken place. We were to leave at 8:00 AM, before the sea got rough. But time there doesn't seem to matter much. Every hour we were told we were going to leave soon, but kept waiting and waiting. At that port, there is nowhere to sit nor is there any shading or covering, so we had to wait outside in the hot sun. We didn't board the boat until 6:15 PM! By then, the sea was very rough. The little boat was tossed up and down for twelve hours with gale winds blowing. I thought it must have been similar to what Paul experienced on the way to Malta. There were screams that could deafen the best of ears. We each sat vomiting into the same bags for twelve hours. I was more concerned for Maria than for myself, thinking the entire time, "What am I going to tell Maria's family if anything happens to her?"

Unfortunately, the boat was not passing close to the island, so right in the middle of the sea, we had to jump out of the boat and into a double canoe for four hours, then into a dinghy for another four hours. Before these last four hours were over, we ran out of petrol right in the middle of the ocean. But praise God they had spare petrol in a drum, which they syphoned into the tank. Thankfully, we eventually did make it to our destination.

The welcome onto the island made the battle of getting there well worth it. We decided to not think about the return trip and just focus on ministering to the people, which was the reason we were there. We were treated like royalty; the people were so friendly and receptive. We had a police escort and radio and TV coverage. Our arrival was televised across the nation.

This island is so remote that if you offended the people, they could say to you, "You are on your own," and you would die there with no one ever knowing. But their hospitality to us was amazing. Those who had beds gave them to us to sleep on and they made their beds on the floor. While we were there, we participated with the leaders in doing reconciliation for the missionaries who had been killed by the nationals. We saw yokes of bondages broken and lives changed by the power of the gospel. That made it worth the challenge of getting there and back to Port Moresby.

I have to tell you that less than two years later, Maria was diagnosed with cancer and died very quickly without having an opportunity for me to say goodbye. It broke my heart, but I know that I will see her again someday.

### Back in Australia: Signs and Wonders

I went to Papua New Guinea from Australia and returned. It was wonderful to be back at home with my family and friends, and also to connect with old ministries as well as new ones. The first new door to open to me was with Catholics; maybe the Lord brought me this opportunity because I had worked in Spain, where it's predominantly Catholic.

I began ministering to Charismatic Catholics once a month. One morning after preaching, I made an altar call and opened the service up for prayer. One of the people I prayed for was a Catholic nun. As I was praying for her, I put my hands under her hands, which were facing up. All of a sudden, gold and oil started to appear in her hands. I felt the Lord was saying that He had anointed her to heal the sick. After that day, I was invited to minister at a Foursquare church. As I was praying for people, again gold and oil appeared in another lady's hands. I felt she too was anointed to heal the sick. So I asked her to go and lay her hands on the pastor's wife. I didn't know why I said that; the pastor's wife was not even in line for prayer. The following Monday, I had a call from the pastor's wife. She asked if she could drop by my house. She came to testify of her healing that she had received the day before. She been waiting for years for deliverance from chronic fatigue syndrome, and after that night, she was completely healed.

I had met a Catholic priest at the Charismatic Catholics' meeting who had been baptized in the Holy Spirit. He would arrange meetings and weekends for me to teach on the Holy Spirit. As the word got out to other parishes, some priests were not happy about it so he had to be pretty low-key about what we were doing. But it was exciting because many who came to those meetings had never been born again. We would lead them to the Lord, and then they would be baptized in the Holy Spirit.

The doors also opened in Melbourne, Australia. We had quite a move of the Spirit in a certain part of the city. I flew there regularly to do meetings. One Saturday night, there was a particular young man who had given his life to Jesus. He came back to church the next morning. As I was ministering, I prophesied over him about the call of God on his life. I didn't know this at the time, but he was wanted by the authorities and had been on the run. The next day, he went to hand himself in. The police officer in charge looked for his name in the computer for forty minutes, but could not find it. The young man told the police officer that he had repented for his sins and had given his life to Jesus. Then he said to the police officer, "I suppose when Jesus wiped away my sins, He deleted the file from the computer too." The officer said, "I guess so, young man. I can't find your record. You are a free man. Go live your life." The young man was over the moon. He asked the pastor if he could call me and tell me himself. I was back in Sydney when he called. I had just been listening to Chris Tomlin's song, "His grace is enough." I was able to confirm that His grace is truly enough, even to wipe away a "police record."

Amazingly, this happened again to another young man in Sydney, who had also been on the run. He came for ministry not knowing the other young man's testimony, nor did I know his story. He told me that after he had been to the police to hand himself in that they could not find his criminal record in the computer. He was also declared a free man. He is now married with three beautiful children. What a merciful God we serve! I am forever grateful for the cross.

During my time ministering in other churches in Australia, I also had opportunities to minister in my own church running the Divine Encounter weekend seminars. People came from all over Sydney and some even came from overseas.

## Ministry on Radio Stations and at Conferences

The Lord has gifted me with an ability to help people enter into a deeper, more intimate fellowship with the Lord through worship, which opens them up to receive inner healing and deliverance from bondages. Sometimes, all it takes is for me to hug them with a mother's hug for their bondages to melt away.

I have seen two Down Syndrome babies healed, four paralytics restored, and blind eyes restored. Twenty-one deaf people have been healed, eight of whom were born deaf, and two who were both born deaf and mute. Two had even been born without eardrums. Seven people were healed of tinnitus. Six people received creative miracles of new knees after being scheduled for knee replacement operations. One lady had multiple operations in her back; the doctor had put metal rods in her back so that she could not walk or bend. She had to get around by using a motorized wheel chair. After prayer, she got up and danced, and was once again able to bend over. I have seen legs and arms grow out, TMJ healed, and many backs, necks, shoulders, and ankles healed.

I was myself miraculously healed in February 2011, when I received creative miracles for my liver and bowel. After I was rushed to the hospital with a lot of pain in my chest and stomach, I had some tests done. The doctor came to my bed and said, "Deborah, we have bad news for you. We did different tests and all of them showed that there are numerous cysts found in your liver and a mass in the colon. We are going to keep you in hospital for nine days while we work out what to do. You will be only able to have clear jelly and water."

When the doctor left my bed in the emergency ward, I took my Bible out of my bag and I said, "Daddy, that is the doctor's report, and I don't receive it. What is Yours? I will only receive Your report." The Lord gave me Deuteronomy 31:6-8, which reads, "Be strong and of good courage, do not fear nor be afraid of them, for the Lord your God, He is the One who goes with you. He will not leave you nor forsake you. He will be with you. He will not leave you nor forsake you, do not fear or be dismayed."

I said, "Thank You, Daddy. Whenever there are worn out parts in my Toyota, they take them out and put new ones in. So I am bringing my body to You, my Maker, to take out the worn out parts and put in new parts. I also ask that You would give me a private room so that I don't have to be in a room where I have to watch people eating for nine days. Thank You Daddy for my private room. I will turn it into a resort of worship." And by His grace, I was given a private room even though I didn't have the money and was without a private health fund.

After nine days, I was taken to the operating room. Before I was given general anesthesia, the specialist with a very sad face said, "Deborah, do you know why you are here? Did Dr. Adrian explain to you?" I said, "Yes, doctor." He gave me the consent papers to sign, and then I was taken into the operating room. Later on, the doctor came into the recovery room with a smile on his face. He kept shaking his head, saying, "I can't understand it. We did different tests. All the tests showed the tumor and the cysts. Well, you must look after yourself very well. I am going to write to your doctor and say there is absolutely nothing wrong with you. I am putting you on a full diet starting tonight. We need to keep you overnight because you had general anesthesia, but if the procedure had been done earlier, I would send you home now. Also, if it weren't a requirement that you come and see me two weeks after being in hospital, I would say that you didn't need a checkup. But you can come and visit me anyway." Two weeks later, I went to his office. He came out to get the file of the next patient. When he saw me, he walked across the room with a big smile on his face. He shook my hand and said, "I will see you soon." When my turn came, I went in. He was still shaking his head. I asked him for a copy of the report. He said, "A copy! No, I will keep a copy and give you the original. You will not need to come and see me again until you are old and needing a doctor. Go and live your life." The things of the Spirit cannot be understood by human reasoning.

The following week, I went to Pastor Bernadette Nahlous's Friday prayer meeting at Voice to the Nations Church. She has been a faithful friend for years and has stood with me in some very difficult times. If she says, "I will pray for you," you can be assured that she will. She is a woman of the Word and of her word. As I walked across the room, one of the prophetic intercessors turned around and said, "Deborah, the Lord has just shown me that He has given you a new liver and a new bowel." Wow, nobody there even knew that I had been in hospital. It was so important for me to hear that. I was still fighting off the symptoms, even though the doctor had given me a clear bill of health. The enemy does not give in easily. In Matthew 4, he even tried a few times to tempt Jesus, just waiting for an opportunity. But, just like Jesus, I didn't give him one.

After that, the Lord opened a door at the Greek radio station where I ministered on Sunday afternoons. It was interesting to minister with some very traditional Greeks. Some struggled a bit having a woman preacher. But God was touching those who were hungry for the things of God. It's amazing the doors the Lord opens when you have a "Yes" to Him in your heart.

CHAPTER 22

# GETTING A TOUCH FROM
# THE LORD

You may be wondering what I am talking about, but I am going to share something funny that I did that resulted in me receiving an anointing. I received the anointing because I was willing to act like a fool to get it, just like David in 2 Samuel 6:14 when he danced before the Lord wearing only a linen ephod.

I was watching God TV when Benny Hinn's program came on. Benny had invited Reinhard Bonnke onto his program. After they finished ministering and lifting up prayer requests, they turned to each other and started imparting anointing to each other. I actually got up from my couch and stuck my head on the TV to catch the overflow of what they were imparting to each other. I said to the Lord, "It would be wonderful to get those two men to lay hands on me and impart what they are imparting to each other. Well, Lord, I am here and I will be the saucer and catch the overflow."

The Lord saw my hunger. Two weeks later, I had a dream that I was in Benny Hinn's meeting, standing before him. He laid his hand on me and anointing oil started flowing from my head to the floor as if he had poured a big jar of oil over me. After that dream,

I received an invitation from Benny's office in Australia saying that he was coming to Sydney to hold a private impartation weekend for pastors. I was over the moon when I read that. I went and he laid hands on me. Only instead of oil pouring over my head, I went flying over four rows of chairs. When I got up, I was so drunk that I could not drive and had to sit in my car until I sobered up a bit.

Two weeks after that, I received an invitation from Reinhard Bonnke to attend his 50th anniversary in ministry at his head office in Orlando. He said that the Lord told him to only invite 50 up-and-coming evangelists and pour into them. It was called "Face-to-face with Reinhard Bonnke." We were coming in from all over the world. When we got there, his staff told us that he spent three months praying for us. We felt like grown-up children who had come home to our mum and dad for Christmas. We had all our meals with him and his wife, and he would teach and talk to us while we ate. He gave us every book and video he had at that time. I was the only one there who had been born in Africa, and he has a big heart for Africa. So whenever we sat down, he and his wife would have me sit between them and they would give me hugs. He even invited me to go and do a crusade with him in Nigeria. It turned out that my son-in-law had to have an urgent operation, so I had to stay home to help my family, as the children were young. But it was incredible to be asked by such a man. Receiving impartation from these mighty men of God marked my life.

## Moved with Compassion

When I was in hospital with my son-in-law, I noticed that there were people who had no one visiting them. There were some visitors who came to see their loved ones, but they came alone and had no one there to offer any support. Some were even alone when their loved ones died. I felt that I could meet the need I saw around me, but was unsure how. I had started praying about it when my friend's husband got sick. It was a touch-and-go situation and my friend needed the support of a faithful friend. We spent a lot of time together, praying and visiting her husband. I would leave them alone to talk when he was awake and not in too much pain, and walk around the hospital praying. I saw that not everyone had this kind of support, but knew that they too needed love, support, and comfort.

After my friend's husband had recovered, I received a letter in the mail, which was an application form for chaplaincy training. I don't even know how they got my address or that they existed. I decided then that I would go and receive training as a chaplain. I did well and started working in two big public hospitals. Now, if a patient asked me to pray for them, no one could stop me. I started seeing four to five people coming to the Lord every day. I loved it. I got to hear untold stories from 70- and 80-year-olds that entrusted me with their special memories. I also got to see people healed physically, emotionally, and spiritually. It was amazing how the presence of God opened up the secrets of their hearts, which had been locked up for most of their lives. How wonderful it was to see them receive the Lord and be filled with peace and joy. I saw that with most people, when they are healed emotionally, the physical healing follows.

The chaplaincy training I received is nationally and internationally recognized. They train you for all areas of life, even disaster relief, so you can be deployed to help in places or countries where there have been disasters and devastations. It is a very intense course, but the benefits of being able to help another human being in such dire need are so rewarding. I love evangelism, and people are much more open when they are in need or have lost their loved ones. They are more aware of the frailty of human life, more aware that a day will come when this life will end.

While I did the chaplaincy training, I was still part of the ministry team in my church, as well as ministering in different places. One day at the hospital, a lady followed me into the corridor and said, "When you finish your morning tea, would you come to my bed too? I was behind the curtain when the lady was telling you her story. I also have a story I have never told anyone, but I feel that I can talk" you about it." So I went back to her bed, where she told me her story. She ended up forgiving the people who had hurt her, freeing her from her pain, and receiving the Lord. I love the way the Lord positions us to pick the fruit when it's ripe.

One day, when I walked into a ward, they said that they just had a Catholic priest visiting with them. I said, "Well then, you don't need me." All the four ladies in that ward said, "Oh yes, you are the one we want. Come in." I ended up leading the four of them to the Lord.

One day while I was doing my rounds, I felt that I should go into one room, but hesitated and walked past it. Before I got into another one, the Lord said, "Go back to the room you just passed." I turned around and went back to find a man in the first bed. When I shook his hand, he grabbed me tight and said, "I am so glad you came back. You are my only hope for help. I was worried that you wouldn't come back after I saw you walk past. I am dying of AIDS and I don't want to go to hell. I know you can help me. Please help me, please!" I said, "Yes, I will help you. You don't have to go to hell if you don't want to. Hell was not meant for people. God doesn't want any of us to go there, but He has given us a free will. You can choose to give your life to Him and go to heaven, or you can choose to rebel against Him and go to hell." He said, "No! I don't want to go to hell." I said, "Okay, I will help you," and I led him to the Lord. After that he started looking up and smiling, as if he could see something. I said to him, "What is it you are seeing up there?" He said, "I see light and I feel light. Thank you so much. Now I know I am not going to hell. I would like my daughter and my wife to know that I am not going to hell." How I wish I had met his wife and daughter to tell them the story. When I went back the next day, he had died and his body had been moved from the ward.

I have many stories of the Lord directing me to different wards and allowing me to see Him meet the people at their point of need. By being obedient to His leading, I saw Him do amazing things. As a chaplain, I had liberty to go to any ward and visit with any patient, visitor, or staff member if they wanted me to pray for them. Sometimes we were even called to pray for doctors and nurses when they had had a traumatic case. One day there was a birth that should have been normal but resulted in a horrific death that nobody was expecting. We were called upon to respond to that situation.

Another story was that of a Muslim man who was dying of cancer. His wife a Catholic lady, worked with my friend from church. She asked if we could go and pray for him. When we arrived, I tried to talk to him about Jesus. He said, "But I am a Muslim." I said, "Jesus loves Muslims too." I told him about God's plan of salvation, and then I led him to the Lord. He was lying in bed looking up and turning his head as if he was seeing something on the ceiling. Then I asked him, "What are you looking at up there, what are you seeing?" With a big smile he said, "I see light and I feel light." I said, "Jesus has taken away the weight of sin from you, eh?" He said, "Yes, oh yes, I see light and I feel light." I said, "You see, Jesus loves you so much." He just smiled and said, "Thank you for coming to see me." I turned to his wife and said, "Wouldn't you like to accept Jesus today too, so that when your husband goes, he will go knowing he is going to see you again in eternity and not have a permanent separation?" She said, "Yes, I would." So I led her to the Lord. That happened on a Sunday afternoon; on Tuesday, her husband went to be with the Lord. My friend and I went to the funeral. His wife said to me, "I am so happy that I know where he is and that I will see him again." She was very grateful for our love and support.

Around this time, I saw a need for single people's ministry in our church and I was praying about it. When I felt it was the right time, I went to my pastor and shared what was in my heart. My pastor said, "I have been praying about that and I felt you were the right person to run that. So I have been praying and waiting for you." Then I realized that it had been in God's heart for me to do it, so we made a date to start and sent out invitations. I have always had a vision for the unity of the Church of Jesus Christ. To my surprise, we had people from seven churches respond. I am a pioneer. From the very start, I began to mentor someone who could take my place.

When I was to come to Bethel, there was no problem finding someone to take over from me.

CHAPTER 23

# HONOR THE PROPHET, RECEIVE THE WORD, WAIT FOR CONFIRMATION

As I mentioned before, our church was in revival in the 1990s. We had preachers and prophets who were on fire coming to minister in our conferences. One of those prophets had prophesied over me that I would get married again and that the Lord would restore all that was illegally taken from me. Like Mary, I pondered the word in my heart and like Abraham I waited for the promise. I had many offers of marriage, but agreed to none of them. I tarried past Father Abraham's waiting time for Isaac. The Lord gave me the grace to stay pure until the promise was fulfilled. Besides, I was busy with the ministry and enjoyed what I was doing; I never had time to be lonely or bored. If you are generous with your love, time, and money, there is no time to be lonely or bored. You actually crave to have your own space and to have time alone for self-care, which you must have for longevity in ministry or even for life in general. If you are going to be in it for a long haul, it's a must-have.

I was enjoying the work I was doing for the Lord. I was invited to speak in Sydney by a friend who was also friends with my spiritual son and his father, Chris. Chris didn't know that I was his son's spiritual mother. When I came to Sydney, I held quite a few meetings. Chris came to all of them and fell in love with me, although I didn't know this. I had two dreams in which he came to my house to pick me up and we went out to minister together. When I woke up, I wondered what that was all about. At the time, I was not thinking of getting married. I was enjoying what I was doing in ministry too much to think about marriage. Without me knowing it, he had a dream too. In his dream we were in an intimate relationship. All this was happening before we ever talked to each other about that kind of relationship. He told his sister that he had fallen in love with me and was going to ask me to marry him. His sister said, "Chris, if she says yes, you will be a very blessed man." His sister went and told their mother, saying, "Chris has fallen in love with a girl of color." His mum said, "I don't mind color as long as Chris is happy. I want him to be happy." Chris and his sister, Linda, are her only children. Again, all of this was going on without me knowing a thing.

I was a chaplain and I knew that he was grieving for the loss of his wife, who died of cancer. I offered him to pick up a couple of books on grief and have something to eat. I was not thinking of anything more; I just wanted to lend him the books. I had already forgotten about the dreams. Anyway, he came to my house. As he was leaving, he said, "Before I go, I would like to say what's in my heart. I have fallen in love with you." Then I said, "Is this why I have had two dreams about you?" He then said, "I had a dream too, about you and me. We were not just friends, we were intimate friends." I just looked at him and smiled. I didn't say a word, but I was thinking, "No way, Jose!" I had no plans for marriage. Life was good with the Lord. I was doing what I loved to do. But from then on, he would offer to pick me up for church and for special meetings and conferences. I was a friend with his pastors before I met him and before he started going to their church. Chris' church is what we call "in the river," because evening services there are full of people coming from other churches to drink from the Spirit. They have many visiting speakers who are "in the river" in the Body of Christ. If you want to experience the presence of God and go deeper in Him, that is one of the most recommended places to go in Australia.

One day, while Chris was visiting with me, his mum rang him. He said to her, "Mum, I am visiting Deborah, the lady Linda told you about. Would you like to say hello to her?" She said, "Yes, I would love to," so Chris handed me the phone. She said, "Hi, Deborah, it's Chris' mum. Please look after my boy, he is a good man." Out of my mouth came, "Yes, Mum, I will." After that, I said to Chris, "What was I going to say to a 94-year-old lady? I didn't want her to die on me by saying no to her." But I think he hung on that and never gave up. He kept pursuing me, offering to pick me up to go wherever I was ministering or to go shopping.

## San Diego AGIF Annual Pastors Conference & Bethel Church, Redding

Every year, the AGIF (Assemblies of God International Fellowship) pastors meet to seek the Lord together for the vision of the year. In 2013, I was invited to come and be a speaker on behalf of Australia. This was my first time to speak in that conference. After I spoke, the leaders wanted to take photos with me and have meals with me, but no one said anything about the word that I brought for the vision.

I had asked the Lord to make a way for me to visit Bethel Church while I was in California. So after the conference, I flew to Redding. I arrived at night and took a taxi to Bethel the next morning. As soon as the taxi entered onto Bethel's property, I started feeling the presence of the Lord. The land was pulsating with life. It felt like everything was alive and breathing. Every bush and blade of grass was on fire, but not burning. Even now, every time I think of it, I experience the presence of God like I did when I first got here. My prayer is, "Lord, please never let me lose the wonder of Your Presence in this place. May I never take it for granted, may I never get so familiar with it that I lose the hunger. So many people long to experience what I am getting everyday." That day, February 2, 2013, was my first visit to Bethel.

Then the next day I attended all of the day services and the evening service. The speaker only spoke for about fifteen minutes then she said, "I can't continue this message until I deliver this word. Is Deborah in the house?" I responded, "Yes, I am." Then I was prophesied over, with the Lord saying, "I am now going to put you on display because of your faithfulness. You are going to be nourished by your faithfulness and more." I didn't know what the Lord meant by putting me on display. When I got home, the AGIF magazine had already arrived. I opened it and on the contents page was: "The vision for AGIF for 2013 on page 12 from Australia," and there was my picture and message on a full page and half. That magazine goes to every nation where AGIF is. Wow, what a surprise for little me!

When I was visiting Bethel, I also received a prophetic word about writing this book. I was very excited as I had had many people say that I should write a book and I had longed to do it. On my second visit, as we were worshiping, I found myself praying, "Lord, it would be nice to come and stay for a while, just worshiping You here with these people." At that time I had not yet heard about the school of ministry and when I did, I didn't think that they took mature students. I thought, "Maybe I can come for one year and write the book." I had no money left for school after a month of holidays in the US. But then I received the prophetic words about God's provision. My first friend at Bethel, Belva Spainhover, was one of the intercessors who had welcomed me on my first visit to the Healing Rooms. She took me to all the people she knew who have "juice" and said, "Pray for this Australian pastor. Give her what we carry in this house. She wants to take it back to her church." By the time they finished with me, I was as drunk in the Spirit as a sailor. The next day, Sunday, she again took me to different leaders who prayed over me. As we were going out of the morning church service, there was a young prophetic man standing at the door who prophesied that the money for school would come in.

When I got back to Australia I asked my senior pastor, Judith Gates, if I could be released to go to Bethel School of Supernatural Ministry. She was very happy for me. It was wonderful to see everyone happy for me, especially since I felt God's favor on it too. So on Monday morning, I applied at 9:00 AM and by 3:00 PM I had my reply. An Aussie pastor interviewed me over the phone and then I was accepted. It was a miracle that it all happened so fast. I did receive the $6,000 that the young man had prophesied I would receive. Then someone gave me $5,000. Then another one gave me $1,000, another $800. More people just started giving me $100 and some $50. In no time at all, I was able to apply for my visa. I was only asked two questions and my five-year visa was granted on the spot. In less than half an hour, my visa was approved. Wow, Daddy, thank You.

I went home and FaceTimed my friends, Doug and Donna. They gave me a number to call about an apartment in Redding. I rang the owner who said they didn't have any vacancies. I asked her if I could give her my email because I didn't need an apartment until the first of September and it was only the end of June. She said, "My husband looks after that, but he is in the hospital. I was hoping he would come home today; I am actually just about to leave to go to the hospital to see him." I said, "Can we pray for your husband?" She hesitated. I said, "I mean, can I pray and if you can, agree with me please?" She said, "Oh yes, I can do that." I prayed just as she had said that she wanted him home. "Lord, Margaret wants her husband home. So I command David's body to be healed now in Jesus' name. When the doctor comes to do his rounds, he will say, 'David, you are better, you can go home now,' and Margaret will bring him home."

And that is what happened. The Lord healed David, and Margaret was able to bring him home that day. There is no distance in prayer. I prayed in Australia and David was in the hospital in California. Do not underestimate the power and authority you have been given by Jesus over the works of the devil. Use it for His glory.

I rang the next day to see how David was doing. Margaret answered the phone and said, "We still don't have an apartment." I replied, "I realize that you wouldn't have an apartment overnight. But I am calling to see how David is doing." She said, "Oh, let me put him on. He came home with me yesterday. It happened just as you prayed. Here he is, you can talk to him." David came on the phone and thanked me for praying for him. Then he took my email address and said that if an apartment became available, he would let me know. In August, while I was driving back from visiting a friend in the hospital who had had a knee operation, I found myself thanking the Lord for my apartment and a car before I had gotten them. I remember saying, "Daddy, thank You for an apartment and a car for Your princess." Since I had already found a tenant for my house, I was staying with my daughter at the time. When I got to her house, I felt that I should look at my emails after dinner. I did and there was one email from David saying, "Deborah, an apartment is going to be ready the day you arrive in Redding; if you still want it, it's yours. The missionaries who were in it have just decided to go back to the mission field. It just gives us enough time to clean it the day before you arrive. We will keep it for you. You can give us the deposit when you arrive." I thought, "Wow, Dad, that is awesome!"

The day that I moved to Redding, I arrived at midnight. I came to the apartment not knowing it was not furnished. My friend, Sandra, had picked me up from the airport she took me to her house for the night. The next day, the Lord gave me favor with Margaret the landlord. She picked me up from Sandra's house because Sandra had to go to work. Margaret took me to her house. She gave me food, sheets, blankets, kitchen utensils, pots, a frying pan, and plates. Then she took me to a furniture shop which another friend had recommended to buy furniture. How awesome it is when the body of Christ takes care of each other.

It was like a mother who was helping her daughter. Instead of me having to pay for a delivery truck (which wouldn't come until the next day), she went back home, brought her pickup, collected the furniture, and took me to my apartment. She asked the neighbor in one of her apartments if he could help arrange my furniture. In three and a half hours, I was all set to start school. It's amazing what favor can do for you. We serve a mighty God. I am so grateful for beautiful friends the Lord has given me.

In December, Chris decided to come to Redding to make sure that someone had not snatched me up at Bethel. He then booked two rooms at the Grand Canyon for the Christmas holidays for us to go to, after which we returned to Redding. He stayed in Redding for a month but went home disappointed. I still was not thinking of getting married. After being single for 27 years, I had learned to be happy on my own. Before school finished, he emailed me and asked if I was going home. I said, "I was thinking of going to Hawaii after graduation." He offered to pay for my holidays, no strings attached, and asked if I would meet him there. Then, just after we graduated first year, I went to the Friday night church service. Ben Armstrong, the Prophetic Ministry Director in Bethel, was the speaker that night. After he was introduced, he said, "Before I speak I would like the whole church to pray with me. There are too many single women in our church. I want us to pray that those who are not thinking of getting married will want to get married, and for those who want to get married, that the Lord will open the eyes of the men to see them." So we prayed. I prayed with all my heart for the women who wanted to get married. I have learned that when a prophet speaks, God wants us to take note. But I never thought of myself as one of the women we were praying for. Even though I had agreed to meet Chris in Hawaii, I was still happy the way I was.

The next day friends from my class had organized a get-to-gether lunch. I had already been invited to another lunch for the

BSSM alumni and afterwards had planned to go to a birthday party. They said, "Deborah, we don't mind if you don't eat; we just want you to come and pray for us." So I went. When I got there, I said, "Can we just worship a little bit first before we pray?" As we worshiped, I got a prophetic word. Before I released it, I knew that it was not just for them, but it was for all of us. Part of the word was, "There are sudden changes coming, good changes, and you are at the cross-roads. You are not to turn to the left or to the right; the Lord will direct your steps and you will rejoice in what is about to take place." (There was more to the prophetic word, but I can't remember it all.) The main thing is that we all received sudden changes and they were indeed good changes. The next week, I flew from Redding and Chris flew from Australia, and we met in Hawaii at the hotel where we would be staying. The hotel staff were shocked to actually see two adults of the opposite sex book separate rooms. They told us that they do not see that in Hawaii. I told them that we were Christians. They said, "Oh yes, we have had Christians here, too, but we have never seen this." We ended up leading two of the staff to the Lord.

One evening, after a few days there at Waikiki Beach, Chris said, "Can we go to the beach?" I said, "Yes, I will come and watch you swim." When we got to the beach, he said, "Can you put a towel here to sit?" I said, "Yes, but I thought you wanted to swim." He said, "Yes, I will later. I just want to sit and talk for a while." We sat down a little while, and then he popped the question, "Deborah, will you marry me?" To my surprise I found myself saying, "Yes, I will marry you, Christopher Charles Benson." Tears of joy welled up in his gentle eyes. We sat there and talked as lovers do and then went to dinner. Right then, Ben Armstrong's prophetic word was fulfilled. The next day, we went to a shop and he bought the rings. He was so excited that he wanted to put the engagement ring on in the shop, but he waited for the evening until we went to a romantic place.

When it was time to leave Hawaii, Chris found it hard to go back to Australia because I was going back to Redding and wouldn't be back in Australia for another two weeks. He had waited over three years for me to say yes and didn't want to wait much longer to get married. When I later arrived in Australia, his sister Linda, and her husband, Wayne, welcomed me into the family. As she was hugging me, Linda said, crying, "Mum would have been so happy to see you marrying my brother." His mum had died while I was visiting Bethel, before I went to BSSM.

When I got back to Redding, I rang my pastor in Australia, Judith Gates, on FaceTime. When she answered the phone, I said, "Are you sitting down?" She said, "Why, are you getting married?" I said, "Yes, I am engaged." She said, "Goody, goody, goody! I want to give you a Christian wedding." I said, "Pastor, you have not even asked me whom I am marrying." She said, "Deborah, I know you. You would have put a lot of thought and prayer into this before you made that decision. Now tell me, who are you marrying? He is not American, is he?" I said, "No." She said, "So who is it then?" I said, "It's Chris Benson and he wants to come to BSSM to do the school." She said, "Goody! Let us take care of your wedding. You make your guest list and tell us what you want; we will do it for you."

The name of our church in Australia is "The Blessing." Truly they live up to their name. Chris and I were so blessed. We only had to turn up at the church ready to say, "I do." Hazel, our daughter, was matron of honor and my spiritual daughter, Vanessa Wong, was my bridesmaid; they both looked stunning. Pastor Russell Gates gave me away while Senior Pastor Judith Gates officiated at the wedding ceremony. My church did everything for us up to the honeymoon. I am so grateful for all the hard work my friends and family at church put into our ceremony. Hazel designed the invitations, the bombonieres for guests, and the table sitting cards. It was a most peaceful, fun-filled, joy-filled, love- and laughter-filled wedding. My Pastors even drove us to our honeymoon suite where we stayed for the night before we flew to Maui in Hawaii for our honeymoon.

When I was in first year, Kris Vallotton, Senior Associate Leader of Bethel Church and cofounder of Bethel School of Supernatural Ministry, shared a testimony in class of a young lady who prayed for her virginity to be restored, and the Lord answered her prayer. Bethel believes that when someone testifies, they are saying, "God, do it again." So I took that testimony for myself. I said, "Lord, I have had three children, but I have lived in purity for 27 years and I am asking You to do it for me too. I have beaten Father Abraham with two years in waiting for the promise. Thank You for restoring my virginity in Jesus' name." I only found out on our wedding night that the Lord had actually restored my virginity. Wow, we serve a good, good Father! After our honeymoon, we flew to Redding for Chris to start first year and me to start second year. At the time of writing this book, Chris just finished second year and I finished third year as an intern.

Chris and I now have had opportunities to go on mission trips together. I am reminded of what happened on the mission trip to Argentina in February 2016. We did a conference and then on Sunday morning, we were divided into teams to go and minister in different churches. In the afternoon, we went and did street evangelism. My companion and I stopped at one house where there was a young man standing outside his house. He was not open to the gospel at all, but we just allowed the love of God to flow through us what I call the ministry of Presence. I shook hands with him and held it a little to let the love flow. All of a sudden, he began to soften towards us. His mother arrived then, but was just as resistant as her son, so I continued to make eye contact with her. Then she said, "There is something different about you two. I see it in your eyes." She was holding my hand and said, "I feel something coming from you." I said, "It is the love of Jesus you are feeling." She then said, "Come into my house." When we went in and sat on the couch with her sitting next to me. I put my arm around her and she started to weep in my arms. She opened her heart and started sharing some things with us. We prayed for her and her family and she then received Jesus as her Lord and Savior. She went from being very resistant to, "Come into my home." As we were entering the house, I remembered what Jesus said, "When you enter a house, speak peace to it. If they receive you, the peace will remain. If they don't receive you, the peace will return to you." I believe the peace remained in that house.

In 2014, we went to Mexico on a mission trip. The night we arrived, we were encouraged to declare what we wanted to see during the trip. I declared that I wanted to see blind eyes open. On the last night of the trip, at the church where we were ministering, there was an older gentleman who was blind. One of the people there called me to pray for him. I did, and his eyes were opened and he could see clearly.

Right here in Bethel, Chris and I have opportunities every week to pray for the sick from all over the world and to see them healed. We evangelize in the city and prophesy over people. It's wonderful how they prioritize marriages and families here. They always put marriage and family first before ministry. When you have healthy families, you will have a healthy church. Jesus died for relationship. God gave His only Son so we could have relationship with Him and the Holy Spirit. I encourage you to open wide your heart to receive Him. If you have not yet surrendered your life to him, I encourage you to do it. You will never regret it. It's the best relationship you can ever have.

# CHAPTER 24

# THE MIRACLE WORKING GOD

The God of the miracles that we read about in the Bible is the same yesterday, today, and forever. He is still in the business of miracles, healing, and deliverance. I love being His hands, feet, and mouth. What you are about to read should stir you up even more to want to tap into the well He has put inside you and let the river flow where it's needed most.

My youngest daughter Hazel had been married about two years. One day in my secret place, the Lord gave me Isaiah 66:9: "Do I bring to the moment of birth and not deliver?" Then Exodus 23:26: "None will miscarry or be barren among you." I pondered on those Scriptures, wondering what it was all about. I was praying and declaring them that there would be no miscarriage and no barrenness among us. A few months later, my daughter found out that she was pregnant, but soon after she started bleeding. She went to the doctor, who told her that she was miscarrying. She rang and told me what was happening. I told her about the Scriptures the Lord had given me months before and that the Lord had already gone before us. I said to her, "Change to a new doctor and I will come with you."

When we went to see the new doctor, I said, "Doctor, I have a covenant with my God and my daughter is not going to miscarry the baby. If you can promise me that you are not going to speak negative words over my grandchild or my daughter, I will let you look after her. Doctor, you see these hands of mine? They are going to nurse this baby. And if you agree, your hands are going to deliver this baby at full term. But if you do not agree, then I will take her somewhere else." The doctor said, "I agree." I said, "Doctor, put it here." I stretched my hand out and shook hands with him. Every time my daughter was due for a checkup, I went with her. She bled on and off for five months, but we continued praying. My son-in-law, George, and I were fasting and praying. The doctor did not say a negative word. The only thing he would say was, "I do not know where the blood is coming from, but the baby is still okay." I said, "Doctor, we are praying and I know our God is keeping this baby safe." I would speak to the baby in the womb and say, "Baby, you are to be bonded to your mum until the fullness of time. We love you, baby, but it's not time for us to see you yet. We are happy to wait for the right time."

One day, George was working in the city of Sydney. He went into an elevator when all of a sudden the Lord filled it with light and said to him, "It's going to be alright." He rang and told me about that. That gave us confidence to keep praying for the next five months. I had told my daughter to call me any time she started bleeding, even in the middle of the night. So it could be 2:00 AM, but I would get into my car and drive to their house and pray with them. One night, Jesus came into their bedroom, filled it with light, and said, "It's going to be alright." Hazel was fast asleep. Jesus' presence was so awesome; George said he could not move to wake her up to see. He hoped that she would wake up to see the light of His presence that filled the bedroom.

Four weeks before the baby was due, Hazel had an ultrasound. It showed that the baby was very small. I told the doctor that we were going to pray, and that the same God who was keeping the baby in there was going to cause the baby to grow to a normal size. I went home and I called my prayer partner to ask the Lord with me for the baby to grow a pound per week. We went for a check-up and the doctor said, "My, my, it's not a small baby in there anymore." In the meantime, the doctor himself was given a bad report about his health and needed an operation. But his own doctor gave him less than a 50 percent chance of returning to his practice. When we went for a check-up, the doctor said to Hazel, "I am not going to leave you in the hands of another doctor. I am going to wait until you have your baby. If you have your baby at midnight, then in the morning I will go in for my operation." I said to the doctor, "My family and I are going to be praying for you. You have been good to us and my Bible tells me that he who blesses us, our God will also bless. I believe that you are going to be alright and you are going to deliver the next two babies that Hazel and George are going to have." (It had been prophesied that George and Hazel where going to have three children.)

It happened exactly as foretold. The baby was born at midnight. The doctor turned to us and asked us to pray for him before he left the room, which we did. He went in for his operation in the morning, which was successful. He told Hazel, "After your babies are here, I am going to retire," and he did. Just before they were born, the next two babies both turned in the womb to be in the breech position. The doctor said, "The position they are in is dangerous for both the mother and baby." I said, "Doctor, give me three days to pray. If nothing happens in three days, then you can do what you have to do." He said, "I give you three days only because the position the baby is in is dangerous for mother and baby." We agreed. In both situations and in less than three days, the babies turned and were born normally. We give God all the glory for His love and mercy to us.

In 2013, I was having a lot of pain in my back, so I had tests done. When the results came in, my doctor said, "The only solution is an operation." I said, "I need a miracle doctor." He said, "I will send you to the best specialist in Sydney who did my father's back," but I said, "Doctor, I am very happy for your father, but for me, there will not be an operation. I want a miracle doctor." He said, "I will send you to the specialist and he will send you for MRI tests, then he may want to give you a cortisone injection first." I said, "Doctor, no cortisone injection for me…a miracle doctor!" He sent me to the specialist anyway. Chris drove me. I could hardly walk because of pain, but we kept praying. The specialist sent me for an MRI. When the results came back, he looked at me and said, "Deborah, you were right. You don't need an operation. Just keep doing what you have been doing, stay as you are, and don't put on weight." You see, God heard my cry and He healed me. He restored the discs that were worn out. His eyes are upon the righteous and His ears are open to their cry (Psalm 34:15; 1 Peter 3:12).

### *I Shall Remember the Deeds of the Lord;*
### *More Miracles and Healing*

I shall remember the deeds of the Lord. I shall surely remember the wonders of old and I will meditate on Your ways and consider Your mighty deeds. Your ways, Oh Lord, are holy. Who is like our God? You view me through eyes of grace, so I am not afraid of Your intimate awareness. I rejoice in You who understands me completely and loves me perfectly. As You fill me with Your love, I become a reservoir of love overflowing into the lives of other people.

On my first trip to Bethel in 2013, my return flight to Australia was cancelled, which gave me another opportunity to visit the BSSM second year class on February 12th. That day, Bill Johnson Senior Leader in Bethel Church came to the class and said, "I was not scheduled to speak today, but the Lord sent me because He wants to mark the people in this room." I thought, "Wow, Lord, You cancelled the plane so that I could be here to get marked." I felt highly favored that the Lord would go to that length. Then when I came back the following year on June 12th, during my last service at

Bethel, Eric Johnson Local Church Senior Leader in Bethel Church repeated, "The Lord wants to mark every person in this room."

The following are some of the testimonies that I previously mentioned:

## 2014

• 18th October 2014: Melissa healed of a deaf ear after 17 years.

• Kelly, an 18-year-old, very angry lady with a broken ankle and a broken shoulder after a car accident, was healed then gave her life to Jesus.

• 8th November 2014: Hans, a man deaf for eleven years, was healed.

• A man with no feeling on one side of his body who looked like a zombie was healed and got his feeling back and was baptized in the Holy Spirit.

• 29th November 2014: In my secret place, I had a vision that everyone I prayed for that day was healed. Then later I prayed for Tom, a 15-year-old boy who was deaf from birth. His ears opened for the first time in his life. His mother and father's jaws dropped as he was telling them that he could hear. This is a miracle I wished I had videotaped.

• 13th December 2014: Rhonda's back was healed and her deaf ears were opened. She was given money to buy hearing aids, but decided to get prayer first. After her ears were opened, she pulled out the bundle of money and said to her daughter, "Come on, baby, let's go shopping," waving the money.

• 14th December 2014: Michelle, a lady in her late 40s, born with one ear deaf and a good ear, which got infected and had gone deaf. I prayed for the infected ear, which was healed and opened. Then I said, "Would you like me to pray for the other ear to hear too?" She reluctantly agreed and I prayed and the Lord opened the ear that had never heard for nearly 50 years. WOW, God!

• A young lady with stomach problems was healed, and gold appeared in her hands as a sign that she was healed. She was a new Christian and had asked God for a sign before I prayed for her. I found out later. She was so excited to see the sign. God truly will meet us where we are.

• 21st December 2014: A man who had been booked for a knee replacement operation received a creative miracle of new knees.

## 2015

• 4th January 2015: A German man was healed of tinnitus.

• 21st January 2015: A 40-year-old who was born with a hernia and always in pain, was healed and the hernia disappeared after I prayed.

• 24th January 2015: A man healed of diabetes had numb feet and hands for ten years. I felt led to run around him, crying out, "Freedom!" As I did, he started weeping as he felt the feeling coming back into his hands and feet.

• 31st January 2015: Natalie was healed of deafness, stress, and tinnitus, which were verified by her doctor.

• A Spanish lady's knee was healed after 17 years of excruciating pain after a surgery that went wrong. Then she had fallen on it and twisted it twice two weeks before she got healed. She had previously lost her husband, son, and grandson all within two years, so she was also healed of a broken heart and grief.

• 25th March 2015: One afternoon in Tijuana, Mexico, while treasure hunting, seven people got saved in 30 minutes and a teenager was healed of deafness.

• 28th March 2015: In Tijuana, on Revolution Street, a murderer and a son of a murderer asked one of the team members to call me down from the platform to pray for him. He said, "I don't want to kill anymore. I know you can help me stop." He got saved and was delivered from demons.

• 29th March 2015: At Laguna Niguel Beach, a man in his 50s, had his twisted, deformed ankle healed which had been that way since he was a little boy, when his father left him and his mum. His broken heart was healed too as he forgave his dad. He was then saved and filled with the Holy Spirit.

• 9th March 2015: A woman, who had had many surgeries and had metal rods in her back and a lot of pain in her back, shoulders, neck, and a broken heart, was healed. She had been getting around in a motorized wheelchair, but was now able to bend down, sit on the floor, and move her arm around, which she had not been able to do for years.

• 12th May 2015: What was lost was restored. My diamond and emerald ring went missing. I called it back to my finger every single day for six months. On the evening of our graduation from first year, I went to my classmate and neighbor, Esther, and asked her to agree with me in prayer. I declared that, "My ring has to come back to me. I am not going back to Australia without it, and no one else is going to wear it." When I went back into my apartment, there it was in the doorway of my walk-in wardrobe. Then twelve months later my eternity ring went missing too. After calling it back for weeks, it was also found and restored back to my finger. God perfects what concerns us.

• 13th May 2015: The deaf ears of Jinni, a Taiwanese lady, were opened after prayer in my apartment, after reading of my testimony in the 2014-2015 BSSM testimony book.

• 16th May 2015: Two women with TMJ were healed.

• A man with legs that were numb from the knees down received feeling.

• A man with kidney failure, who was not able to pass urine for two years and had a lot of back pain, was healed. After praying for him, he went to the bathroom and passed urine naturally.

• 6th June 2015: A woman with metal in her back after surgery who could not bend or walk was able to leap for joy after receiving her healing.

• A man had had both his knees broken and had suffered with excruciating pain for nine years. The pain tablets were not strong enough to numb the pain. He received a creative miracle of new knees. I said, "Dad, send an angel with a pair of knees." Then I prophetically touched his knees and said, "Here you are." He started jumping up and down praising the Lord, pain free.

• A lady with floaters in her eyes was healed.

• 7th June 2015: A lady with a degenerative disease and a dislocated hip and knee, and wearing a knee band to keep the joint together, was healed of her pain.

• 7th December 2015: At 10:15 AM, a BSSM student who was born without an eardrum received a new eardrum.

• 11th December 2015: At 9:00 PM, a 55-year-old woman in a coffee shop was healed, both physically and emotionally. She had been deaf and mute from birth.

## 2016

• 2nd January 2016: A boy was healed of autism and stuttering.

• 18th May 2016: I led a young German man to the Lord at the gate of God's Acre cemetery of the Moravians in Herrnhut in Germany, in front of Von Zinzendorf and his family's graves. Straight after that, a man came to us with a lot of pain in the knee, and the pain left after praying for him.

• 24-29th May 2016: My husband and I stayed in the home of Evan Roberts, revivalist during the Welsh revival of 1904, and slept in his bedroom. At Moriah Chapel, Loughor, we met a godly man who knew Evan Roberts in person. His uncle was Evan Roberts's friend; he used to go with his uncle to Evan's house when he was a boy. WOW, God, thank You for favor.

• 29th May 2016: We went to George Muller's homes in Bristol, England, where orphans were brought up by faith without him ever asking anyone for money. He would sit the children at the table, give thanks, and piping hot food would appear at the door.

• 26th May 2016: We went to the college of Rees Howells, the intercessor. He was a powerful man of prayer who greatly influenced the war between the Allies and Germany through his intercession.

• 30th October 2016: During "Awakening Europe" in Sweden, a young lady from Norway was healed in the restaurant after injuring her shoulder and back falling down 7 meters.

• 10th November 2016: I led a 90-year-old man to the Lord. After praying for him, he said, "I feel like I have just had a bath, I feel so clean." He is a lovely gentleman and is always very happy to see me.

• 19th November 2016: A man booked for knee replacement surgery received a creative miracle of two new knees. He was weeping with gratitude to the Lord.

## 2017

• 14th January 2017: A 29-year-old lady born with something wrong with her feet, which resulted in her being in pain all the time, was healed after I prayed for her.

• A lady came very distressed after being told she couldn't have babies. She had tinnitus and pain in her back and shoulder. I prayed for her ears first and the tinnitus left. Then I felt led to command the pelvic bones to rotate into divine alignment. When I did that, there was a shift that took place. She said, "I felt it," and I saw her body shift. Then all her pain was gone. It's so wonderful when we get the Holy Spirit's instructions right.

• 11th February 2017: A man who injured his shoulder 43 years prior was healed after praying for him. He was weeping with joy.

• A woman who had numb fingers and pain in her arm for five years was healed.

• A woman with vertigo and painful shoulder was healed. (I had a word of knowledge of vertigo before I knew I was going to be praying for someone with it.)

• A man who said he was a pastor was healed of tinnitus and backache. I asked him to look into my eyes, and as he did, demons threw him onto the floor. I cast out the demons. He said, "Wow, that was a mighty deliverance, I am free at last. Thank you so much."

• 17th February 2017: A man booked for knee surgery and in a lot of pain came struggling to walk down the stairs. He was healed after I prayed for him. He went to the doctor, who said, "You don't need surgery. All you need to do is lose weight." Praise the wonderful name of Jesus our Healer.

• 25th February 2017: A lady from Switzerland was healed of sinusitis and varicose veins.

• 3rd March 2017: We experienced God's favor on our California home. When we went for the house inspection, the lady of the house told us that they didn't know why they were keeping the house until we got there. They had refused two offers that were much higher than ours. With the house, they also included expensive curtains and household goods that we needed. It was our miracle house.

• 28th April 2017: Bonita was healed of excruciating pain in her legs and feet. When Randy saw Bonita healed on the bus, he accepted prayer and his whole left side that had been paralyzed after a stroke five years before was healed. He kept checking his left hand finger movements, as he had been a saxophone player before the stroke and was now able to play again.

UNDER HIS WINGS

## *The Spirit of Creativity Will Flow Through You*

In the midst of writing this book, I started learning how to paint. One of the paintings I did was of the river of Ezekiel. I wanted to paint the river of Ezekiel to remind me that Jesus has given me rivers of living water that overflow with life that can change lives and situations wherever I allow them to flow. A lot of times, it's not the words I speak but it's just through the act of hugging people that God releases His love, and people break down weeping as the emotional pain leaves them. The more I soak in His presence, the more the rivers flow freely. Sometimes I am not even aware of the circumstances people are in. But as I hug them, allowing the rivers to flow, I know when I need to let the rivers overflow more than just giving a hug. It's then that God meets them at their point of need. The longing of my heart and prayer is that wherever these rivers flow, everything that is withered will be refreshed, and what is dead will come to life. My prayer for you is that you will let the rivers flow through your life.

I was given a prophetic word in 1991 that the Spirit of creativity would flow through my hands: "God will take these hands, and you will gently nurse people through their times of crisis." I have seen God do it time after time. But it wasn't until October 2016 that I felt that it was time to step up in creativity and do what I had never done before. I had never drawn a picture or tried to paint anything, but I gave myself permission to try and fail. I had to ask, "Lord, when did I stop being creative? When did I allow the voice of the enemy to stop me? When did I decide that I was not born creative? Lord, let this be a restoration time of creativity and dreams.

After my first painting of a lion, I felt something was missing, which I told my art teacher. She told me to bring it to class the following week. The night before class, the Lord gave her a dream about my painting. In the dream, she and a man were floating above me. He asked her why she didn't let me put black on it; it would look good. She told me the dream and then advised me to add black. That was all that was needed to complete it.

A life of creativity is fun and satisfying for a number of reasons: it brings rest (as God rested after creating the world), it helps to shape your identity, it produces vitality, and it changes the world. Don't let the enemy steal your future. Don't let fear and disappointment stop you. What you create and invest in today has the potential to create and change your future. Don't rob yourself of your future or let the enemy shut your future down. Look for someone who will laugh with you so you will feel safe when you make a mistake. My art teacher laughs when I make a mistake, although I am panicking. She tells me that the secret of becoming an artist is learning how to correct your mistakes.

### *Thankfulness is the key to heavenly bliss*

Thank You, Daddy, for my art teacher who pulled out the creativity that I didn't know was in there. Thank You, Daddy, for my first year Revival Group Pastor Barbara Kealiinohomoku for her continuous care for my husband and me, especially in helping us buy our California home.

I give thanks to You Oh God
I give thanks to You Oh God I give thanks
For Your wondrous works declare Your name is near
I give thanks
I give thanks
I will declare Your glorious miracles
Take joy my King in what You hear
For the nations which You have made shall come and worship You
Oh Lord, I glorify Your name
Oh that men may give thanks to You oh Lord for Your goodness,
For Your mercy endures forever

What god is great like our God
Who gives and gives
When You died on the cross You held nothing back

Lord, I thank You for all the people you have used to enrich my life. My mouth shall speak the praises of the Lord and all flesh shall bless His holy name forever and ever. I will bless Your name forever!

Lord, I give you all the glory for Your mercy, Your great faithfulness, and for all the things You have done through all these years. I will praise You as long as I live!

Thank You, Daddy, that Your eyes search to and fro through the earth looking for the one whose heart is seeking You. You see me longing to find You and You monitor my efforts and attempts to behold Your Face. Thank You that You are pleased with my desire to create a quiet space where You and I can meet. I know that our mutual search results in joyful fulfillment. I am not discouraged by the difficulty of achieving this goal. For I know that in You I am complete and I have everything. It is impossible for me to have a need that You cannot meet. You have promised to meet all my needs according to Your glorious riches. Your blood has set me free. I give You my worship and all my devotion. Oh, how I love You. Let Your Presence overtake my heart. My heart belongs to You. All I am is Yours. Your grace never ends. Let Your Spirit overwhelm me. My deepest and most constant need is for Your peace. Thank You that You have planted Peace in the garden of my heart where You live, but sometimes weeds grow there, too.

I thank You, Daddy, for You are the Gardener and You work to rid my heart of those weeds when I sit quietly with You. You created me, and everything that is in the world. I refuse to be fooled by things that are visible because they are temporary; the things that are unseen are everlasting. My capacity to experience You is increasing through Your removal of debris and clutter from my heart. As my yearning for You increases, other desires are gradually lessening as You shine the light of Your Presence directly into my heart. In this glorious light, peace increases abundantly and weeds dry up and die. I trust You in the midst of trials. The peace the troubles produce is greater than the suffering I endure, and they bring me forth like gold.

Thank You, Daddy, that You are infinite and abundantly accessible to me. Desiring You above all else is the best way for me to live. I am learning to live above circumstances and accept each day just as it comes and find You in the midst of it all. I know that in the midst of difficulties, You are near. You are my support. In the darkness, You are my light; yes, there is no darkness that the world can produce that can hide Your face from the eyes of faith. In failure, Your encouragement is most welcome. In loneliness, the touch of Your presence is tender. You know no limitations. You always have a fresh supply. I let my heart run wild after You. I am crying out for more. I am crying for a greater measure. You are everything my heart wants. I rejoice and face each day with joy. You have planned ahead for me and made all necessary arrangements. I put my hand in Your hand.

I remember all You have done and how far You have carried me. You are faithful and Your mercy has no end. You have never let me go, You have brought me closer to You. You lead me with Your secret wisdom. And following You brings me into Your brightness and glory. You are all I want. You fill me with love, joy, and peace. As long as I have You, life on earth has nothing more I desire. When I trust in You I have a strong and glorious presence protecting and anointing me. You are all I ever need, forever. I will keep coming closer and closer to You, Lord God.

Daddy, I trust You in every facet of my life. I know that every failure, shortcoming, and mistake will be recycled into something good through Your transforming grace. I will love You through all eternity. I will tell all of Your mercy and Your grace.

I have built an altar that only You Jesus can light the fire. You are the only God who answers by fire. Oh consuming fire let it burn in me until I am aglow with Your living presence, shining brightly in this dark world. It doesn't matter what I used to be; I have found my victory in You, Jesus. It doesn't matter how I feel. Oh, victory belongs to You, Jesus. You have taught me that being sold out to You is the only way acceptable to live. As I snuggle under Your wings, I am not only discovering refuge, I am also finding an increasing ability to trust You. It's in the closeness to You that I am becoming more aware of the love You poured out and how trustworthy You are.

Jesus, only You will keep me burning until I become a flame of fire that lights many fires, as I contend for breakthrough, for the impossible that only You can do. I thank You for the blood. Your love has freed me as I seek Your kingdom. I know that the strength of Christianity is not outward laws, but inward character. Lord, dwell in my heart through Your Spirit; strengthen me and imprint Your nature upon my mind, will, and emotions. I know You can make something beautiful out of this little life. When I came to the end of myself, You showed up and rescued me. As I give myself to Your ways, Your Spirit swells within me and I am saturated with divine presence and You fill me with inexpressible heavenly joy. You don't make mistakes. Your love is undeniable. I don't try to understand it. My soul says "Yes, I am Yours, Jesus." There is no substitute for You. I am in love with You. I am grateful for Your mercy and grace. Your presence is all I want.

There are some things in life that people can't help. There are some things you cannot get until you get in the presence of God. Daddy, I am seeking You. Let me see Your lovely face. In Your presence is fullness of joy. You have pledged Yourself with covenant faithfulness to respond–all these things shall be added to You. All the glory and the honor belong to You, Jesus.

Let the rivers of living water flow through me. I want the joy of being as close to You as I can be. I make it my aim to please You; I am ruined for anything else. You are worthy of all my praise. There is no one like You, Lord. There is no other god as glorious as You. Step by step, You will lead me and I will forever praise You!

# CHAPTER 25

# TALKING TO JESUS, THE LOVER OF MY SOUL: THE MIRACLE WORKER

Allow me to pause for just a minute or two to talk to the Lover of my soul.

Jesus, You loved and saved us all

Thank You that my past does not exclude me from this love

Thank You, Lord, that this love includes everyone

This love has taken me in and has cast away all fear

I have tasted and seen that You are good

Thank You, Lord, for You take care of me when I am on the mountaintop or in the valley, when I am in want or in plenty

You are my good Shepherd; You have a resting place for me in Your love

You have laid a banqueting table for me before my enemies

I want to walk with You every moment

I want my eyes and my ears open to see and hear You

I am committed to walk in Your truth, to love Your ways, and to

obey Your commands
I hold nothing back; You are the safest place I can ever be
Your love has put my feet on the Rock, a firm foundation
This love has broken every chain and opened every prison door
I want to know You more than I know a best friend
Jesus, I want to shine so that Your glory will be seen upon me
Jesus, I want to be the burning one and a shining light (John 5:35)
I don't want to conform; I want to stand out and be counted
I was not created to fit in, but to be cut above and soar like an eagle
To my knees I fall and listen to You singing over me
(Zephaniah 3:17)
Thank You, Lord, that when I called You came running with open
arms and rescued me
You healed my heart
Search me, oh God, and know my heart, see if there is any wicked
way in me and lead me in the way everlasting;
I want to be closer to You
You have been faithful over the years and I know that You will
never let me down
You are faithful even when I fail You
Thank You, Lord, for Your grace and for where You are taking me
Thank You that You are praying for me, as you did for Peter so that
my faith may not fail
You are interceding for me day and night at the right
hand of the Father
I rest in Your embrace and diligently hearken to Your voice
Thank You, Lord, that You knit me in my mother's womb
You saw good in me when nobody else did
You wrote down in Your book the number of days allotted to me
Father, because I know You, I have set my love upon You
I will live to a full good old age like a shock of grain
Thank You, Lord, for helping me to give up control
I have made up my mind and I'm never going back
You are the center of my life

I am not an orphan
You place the solitary into families
I don't have to strive to find my place in Your heart
I don't have to be good enough; You have invited me to come con-
fidently into Your bright presence
Your blood continually cleanses me from all sin
All I can say is, thank You, Lord. I just want to thank You
I eat and I am satisfied
I refuse to have a broken spirit
You have healed all my wounds and restored my health
I know the path that You have called me to travel is exquisitely
right for me
I will hope continually and praise You yet more and more; my
mouth shall tell of Your righteousness and Your salvation
all the day long
Thankfulness keeps me from complaining and criticizing
When I look at what You have done, I am overwhelmed
You lifted me out of despair and set me down on a firm foundation
I delight greatly in You, Lord; my soul rejoices in YOU my God,
for You have clothed me with garments of salvation and arrayed me
in a robe of righteousness
You have called me Your own
I am undone as I look back and see where You have brought me
from and think of what You have done in me
I will live long and strong and declare Your strength to this genera-
tion, Your power to everyone who is to come
You have revealed to me Your abundance of peace and truth
Your word brings life to my mortal body
Your Son has set me free
Jesus, You have anointed me to do good, heal the sick, and deliver
those who are oppressed by the devil
Overwhelming victory is mine through You, Jesus
You make me strong and guard me from the evil one
The devil's schemes will not defile me

I am dead to sin
My past does not determine my future or my destiny, which You have redeemed
I will not allow the past, shame, guilt, fear or hopelessness to hold me back
You took away my pain and shame
You reached down, kissed my forehead, and said, "I love you, child"
My heart has been filled with peace and joy
I am in love with You, Jesus
I accept Your grace and mercy
I feel secure in Your arms of love and there is no place that I'd rather be
I want You more than anything
Thank You for rescuing me
Thank You for Your faithfulness, Your goodness, and Your mercy
I give myself to You; I give it all to You
I am intoxicated by the kisses of Your mouth
I feel so secure in Your love, that I am never again to be alone
Empty my heart of everything that is false
Feed my soul with the measure of prosperity that pleases You
Don't let the riches of this world replace my need for You
May my satisfaction be found in You
May my teachings be filled with wisdom and kindness
May loving instructions pour out of my lips
May I become a radiant woman and an example to my generation and those still to come
Thank You, Lord, for the joy I can never master
You are closer than the breath I breathe; I will ever praise You
Thank You for paying the price for my freedom
Thank You for restoration
Thank You, Lord, for doing the impossible
Thank You, Lord, that You did it all and that there is nothing to add to the work accomplished by Your blood
Thank You, Lord, that You want to inhabit all my moments, grac-

ing my thoughts, words, and behavior

Thank You, Lord, that as I acknowledge You in all my ways, You will make my path straight

Thank You for breaking me out

Thank You for changing my mindsets

Thank You for never forsaking me

Thank You for giving me joy unspeakable, full of glory that only comes from You

You gave me the oil of joy for mourning, a garment of praise for the spirit of heaviness

Thank You, Holy Spirit, for doing what only You can do

My King and my God, I could sing of Your love forever

Help me to nurture this gift of intimacy within the light of Your presence

Help me to be acquainted with You, so that good will come to me and that I will decree a thing and see it established (Job 22:21-30)

Thank You that Your divine power has given me everything I need for my life

You have given Your very great and precious promises so that I may participate in the divine nature and escape the corruption in the world caused by evil desires (2 Peter 1:3-4)

Thank You for helping me to surrender what I could not keep to gain what I cannot lose

I want to know Your heart we are one

I want my spirit to be entwined with Your Spirit until Your desires are mine

Lord, You said, "Seek My face." My heart says, "Lord, Your face I will seek."

Through Your resurrection I have been born again to an ever-living hope

Help me to remain hopeful no matter what is going on in my life

Jesus, You are my only adequate source of help

The hope You provide is an anchor for my soul, firm and secure even in the most tempestuous water

Thank You that You are constantly working to transform my life
There is no limit to what Your great power and glory can accomplish
You can change the most hopeless situation into outright victory
Thank You that those who hope in You will never be disappointed
Lord, help me to recall that You are able to do more
than I can imagine
Help me not to try and direct Your ways, but to seek to attune
myself to what You are already doing
I know that I am loved, that I belong to You and am secure
I am bold and courageous
I am not afraid
I am not dismayed
I am not disappointed
I am not discouraged
I am not despairing
I have no doubt
I am full of faith
I am significant
You have made me powerful
I believe that You are never going to leave me nor forsake me
I have fled to You for refuge and You are never going to let me down
I have confidence in Your oath and the promises You have given
I am perfectly secure that You are never going to change Your
mind
I never want to take my relationship with You for granted
Abba, Your goodness will never end
It's impossible for You to lie
I hold on to the hope that lies ahead
Jesus, Your love is matchless and beautiful; I am ruined for the ordinary
Your glory is what I long for; nothing else matters
My deepest longing and desire is to sit at Your feet, delight Your
heart with worship, and give You all the glory
I love You, Jesus, with all that I am
My heart and soul are Yours, and You are all I hope to be

This hope is a strong and trustworthy anchor for my soul; it leads me through the curtain into Your sanctuary, where You have already gone for me

You have become my eternal High Priest

Your love and goodness are like the waves, one after the other crashing over me, never letting me go

*In Closing*

As you have read my life story, my prayer for you is that it will become your heart's deepest desire to burn for Jesus and to please Him who did not hold anything back, on the cross of Calvary for the redemption of humanity.

**Prayer of Impartation:** I pray that you will never take your relationship with God for granted, but you will forget about the past and become a man or a woman of intimacy with God in prayer. That Jesus will be your one thing and you will have unquenchable hunger for the Word of God and have one on one times with Him. There you will discover more and more of who He is and what He is saying to you. I pray that you will receive an understanding heart. That will change your inner being. The meaning of His words will release within you revelation to reign in life. I pray that you will build your spiritual life in a way that receives a heavenly reward. I pray for sensitivity to pickup the frequencies of the Holy Spirit, to hear His voice, talk with Him and experience His presence at any time. I pray that you will never let your fire die down but keep it burning (Leviticus 6:9,12-13). The fire must be kept burning at any cost no matter what is going on around you. I pray that you will find that worship is the password or the gateway to the throne of God, to the heart of God, to the glory of God. Praise Him until worship comes. Then worship Him until the glory comes. When we see Him face to face, there will be nothing left to do but worship Him.

71927440R00113

Made in the USA
San Bernardino, CA
21 March 2018